The Global Mindset:

A Roadmap to Intercultural Competence in Business

WILLIAM E HAMILTON JR

CONTENTS

1 INTRODUCTION TO INTERCULTURAL COMPETENCE IN BUSINESS

Defining Intercultural Competence

 In today's interconnected and globalized world, intercultural competence has become essential for business professionals. As diversity and inclusion officers, it is crucial to understand and promote the importance of intercultural competence within organizations. This subchapter aims to provide a comprehensive definition of intercultural competence and its significance in the business realm.

Intercultural competence is effectively navigating and communicating across diverse cultural contexts. It encompasses a range of skills, knowledge, and attitudes that enable individuals to interact respectfully, adapt to different cultural norms, and build meaningful relationships with people from various backgrounds. It goes beyond mere tolerance or appreciation of differences, focusing on developing a deep understanding and appreciation of diverse perspectives.

In today's globalized marketplace, businesses are increasingly operating across borders, collaborating with international partners, and serving diverse customer bases. Intercultural competence is crucial for professionals to navigate these complex environments and achieve their business goals successfully. By understanding the cultural nuances and adapting their communication styles, business professionals can build trust, foster collaboration, and create mutually beneficial relationships.

Intercultural competence encompasses several key components. Firstly, it involves self-awareness and understanding of one's own cultural biases, values, and assumptions. This self-awareness allows professionals to recognize and challenge their biases, facilitating more inclusive and effective communication.

Secondly, intercultural competence involves knowledge of different cultural practices, customs, and communication styles. This knowledge enables professionals to adapt their behavior and communication strategies to better connect with individuals from different cultural backgrounds.

Thirdly, intercultural competence emphasizes empathy and respect for cultural differences. It encourages professionals to approach interactions with an open mind, embracing diversity and valuing different perspectives. By demonstrating empathy, professionals can help build trust and foster inclusive environments that promote collaboration, innovation, and desired business results.

Lastly, intercultural competence requires individuals to develop effective communication and conflict resolution skills. This includes active listening, non-verbal communication, and the ability to navigate cultural differences respectfully for positive outcomes.

In summary, intercultural competence is vital for business professionals operating in today's globalized world. It enables individuals to navigate diverse cultural contexts, build meaningful relationships, and drive business success. As diversity and inclusion officers, it is essential to promote the development of intercultural competence within organizations, fostering inclusive environments that embrace diversity and empower employees to succeed in multicultural settings.

To help promote culturally responsive practices, diversity, equity, inclusion, and belonging in your organization, contact your nearest intercultural development inventory (IDI) qualified assessor (QA) today for an individual or group assessment. The assessment measures where the individual or group is on an intercultural development continuum (IDC). Following the assessment, individuals and groups are debriefed, and intercultural development plans (IDP) are formulated for improvement. Continued coaching is available. The assessments are available for individuals, educational institutions, small businesses, and corporations. Contact your IDI QA or visit https://www.idiinventory.com today!

Importance of Intercultural Competence in the Business World

In today's interconnected global marketplace, navigating and understanding different cultures is crucial for success in the business world. Intercultural competence holds immense importance, as it enables professionals to effectively communicate, collaborate, and build relationships across diverse cultural backgrounds. This subchapter sheds light on the significance of developing intercultural competence in business, specifically targeting diversity and inclusion officers and business professionals seeking to enhance their intercultural skills for business impact.

Intercultural competence refers to understanding, appreciating, and adapting to different cultural norms, values, and behaviors. It goes beyond mere tolerance and requires individuals to engage actively with others from different cultural backgrounds. In the increasingly globalized business landscape, companies are expanding their operations across borders, leading to diverse teams and clients. Intercultural competence helps professionals navigate these multicultural environments, fostering effective communication, conflict resolution, collaboration, and alignment with the strategic objectives and vision.

One of the key reasons why intercultural competence is essential in the business world is its impact on relationship building and corporate values. Cultivating relationships with clients, partners, and colleagues from different cultures is crucial for establishing trust, credibility, and long-term success. By demonstrating an understanding and appreciation for cultural differences, professionals can avoid misunderstandings, miscommunication, and potential conflicts, building strong and lasting partnerships supporting the organization's vision.

Moreover, intercultural competence is vital in promoting diversity and inclusion within organizations. By embracing different cultural perspectives and practices, businesses can harness the power of diversity to drive engagement, innovation, creativity, and problem-solving. Inclusive workplaces that value and celebrate cultural differences attract and retain top talent from diverse backgrounds, enhancing the overall competitiveness and adaptability of the organization.

Additionally, intercultural competence enables professionals to navigate the complexities of global markets. Understanding cultural nuances, local customs, and business etiquette is essential when expanding into new markets or engaging with international clients. It ensures that businesses adapt their products, services, and marketing strategies to meet diverse customer segments' specific needs and preferences, leading to increased customer satisfaction, value, and market share.

In conclusion, developing intercultural competence is paramount for success in the contemporary business world. It empowers professionals to effectively engage with individuals from different cultural backgrounds, fostering strong relationships, driving innovation, and navigating diverse markets. By prioritizing intercultural competence, businesses can build inclusive and culturally intelligent organizations aligned with a vision that thrives in today's global marketplace.

The Role of Diversity and Inclusion Officers in Developing Intercultural Competence

In today's globalized business landscape, diversity and inclusion have become critical aspects of organizational success when aligned with the vision. The ability to navigate and excel in diverse cultural contexts is no longer a bonus but a necessity for business professionals. This subchapter explores the indispensable role of diversity and inclusion officers in helping to develop intercultural competence within organizations in collaboration with Human Resources (HR), business units (BU), and talent development (TD) initiatives.

Diversity and inclusion officers are at the forefront of fostering an inclusive work environment that values and leverages diversity. They are crucial in promoting cultural awareness, understanding, and empathy among employees. By recognizing and appreciating the unique perspectives and experiences of individuals from different cultural backgrounds, diversity and inclusion officers help create a platform for intercultural competence development and alignment with the vision.

One of the primary responsibilities of diversity and inclusion officers is to coordinate the design and implementation of training programs that enhance intercultural competence in alignment with the vision. These programs aim to equip employees with the knowledge, skills, and attitudes to engage with individuals from diverse cultures effectively. By providing opportunities for cross-cultural learning and collaboration, diversity and inclusion officers contribute to developing a global mindset among business professionals.

Moreover, diversity and inclusion officers serve as change agents within organizations. They advocate for diversity and inclusion initiatives, ensuring that they are integrated into various aspects of the business, such as recruitment, talent development, and decision making processes. By championing diversity and inclusion, these officers create an environment where intercultural competence is valued and celebrated.

5

Diversity and inclusion officers also play a crucial role in assessing and addressing potential cultural conflicts within organizations. They facilitate open dialogues and mediate disputes, helping to bridge cultural gaps and foster understanding. Through their expertise in intercultural communication, diversity and inclusion officers promote productive and harmonious relationships among colleagues with diverse cultural backgrounds.

In conclusion, diversity and inclusion officers are instrumental in developing intercultural competence within organizations. Their role in creating an inclusive work environment, facilitating training programs, advocating for diversity and inclusion, and mediating cultural conflicts is crucial for the success of business professionals in today's globalized world. By embracing the expertise of diversity and inclusion officers, organizations can foster a culture of intercultural competence, enabling their employees to thrive in diverse cultural contexts.

2 UNDERSTANDING CULTURAL DIMENSIONS

Cultural Dimensions and their Impact on Business

Understanding and navigating cultural dimensions is crucial for success in today's globalized business world. This subchapter will delve into cultural dimensions and explore their profound impact on business practices and results. This knowledge is essential for diversity and inclusion officers and professionals seeking to develop their intercultural competence for business.

Cultural dimensions refer to the various aspects of culture that shape individuals' behavior, values, and beliefs within a society. These dimensions include but are not limited to power distance, individualism versus collectivism, masculinity versus femininity, uncertainty avoidance, long-term versus short-term orientation, and indulgence versus restraint. Each dimension influences how people interact, communicate, and make decisions within their cultural context.

The impact of cultural dimensions on business cannot be overstated. For diversity and inclusion officers, understanding these dimensions is vital for designing inclusive strategies that respect and value different cultural norms. By recognizing and accommodating cultural differences, organizations can foster a more inclusive work environment and facilitate better collaboration among employees from diverse backgrounds.

Moreover, cultural dimensions shape various aspects of business operations, such as leadership styles, negotiation tactics, decision-making processes, and even marketing strategies. For instance, hierarchical leadership structures may be more prevalent in cultures with high power distance, while in cultures with low power distance, a more egalitarian approach may be favored. Similarly, understanding the degree of individualism versus collectivism in a particular culture can guide marketing campaigns to resonate with the target audience's values and preferences.

Intercultural competence for business professionals relies heavily on understanding and adapting to cultural dimensions. Professionals with this competence can navigate diverse cultural landscapes more effectively, build strong relationships with clients and colleagues from different cultures, and seize opportunities in global markets. By embracing cultural diversity and being sensitive to cultural nuances, these professionals can bridge gaps, avoid misunderstandings, and foster mutual respect and collaboration across cultures.

In conclusion, cultural dimensions significantly impact business practices and desired business results. Recognizing and understanding these dimensions is essential for diversity and inclusion officers and professionals seeking intercultural competence for business. By incorporating cultural dimensions into their strategies, organizations can create inclusive environments. At the same time, professionals can navigate cultural landscapes with finesse, ultimately leading to successful global business interactions in alignment with the strategic objectives and vision.

Hofstede's Cultural Dimensions Framework

In today's globalized business landscape, diversity and inclusion have become crucial factors in ensuring success and competitiveness. As Diversity and Inclusion Officers, your role is to foster a culture of intercultural competence within organizations. Understanding and applying frameworks that can provide insights into cultural values and behaviors is essential to achieving competence. One such framework that holds immense value is Hofstede's Cultural Dimensions Framework.

Developed by renowned social psychologist Geert Hofstede, this framework offers a comprehensive tool to analyze and understand cultural differences. It consists of six dimensions that capture the fundamental aspects of a culture: Power Distance, Individualism vs. Collectivism, Masculinity vs. Femininity, Uncertainty Avoidance, Long-Term Orientation, and Indulgence vs. Restraint.

Power Distance refers to the extent to which less powerful members of a society accept and expect unequal power distribution. Understanding this dimension is crucial for organizations to navigate hierarchical structures and leadership styles in different cultures. For instance, decision-making may be centralized in high power distance cultures, whereas in low power distance cultures, it may be more decentralized.

Individualism vs. Collectivism reflects the degree to which individuals prioritize personal goals over collective goals. Organizations must grasp this dimension to manage teams and foster collaboration across cultural boundaries effectively. Individualistic cultures emphasize autonomy and personal achievements, whereas collectivist cultures prioritize group harmony and loyalty.

Masculinity vs. Femininity pertains to the distribution of roles and values between genders. It helps organizations comprehend the varying expectations and behaviors related to work, success, and gender roles.

Masculine cultures value competitiveness and achievement, while feminine cultures emphasize cooperation and quality of life.

Uncertainty Avoidance focuses on a society's tolerance for ambiguity and unknown future situations. Organizations must acknowledge this dimension to adapt their communication and decision-making processes in different cultures. High uncertainty avoidance cultures may have strict rules and prefer structure, while low uncertainty avoidance cultures may be more open to change and risk-taking.

Long-Term Orientation explores the extent to which a society values long-term goals, such as perseverance and thrift, over short-term gratification. This dimension assists organizations in understanding cultural values related to planning, patience, and delayed gratification. Is thinking about preparing for the future highly valued or not?

Indulgence vs. Restraint measures the extent to which a society allows gratification of basic human desires. Recognizing this dimension helps organizations tailor their marketing strategies and adapt to local consumer preferences.

By familiarizing themselves with Hofstede's Cultural Dimensions Framework, Diversity, Equity, Inclusion, and Belonging (DEIB) Officers can enhance their intercultural competence and guide organizations in navigating the intricacies of global business impacting the desired business results. This framework offers valuable insights into how cultures differ, enabling professionals to bridge gaps, align strategy, build meaningful relationships, and ultimately drive business success in diverse environments toward achieving the vision.

Trompenaars' Cultural Dimensions Framework

Diversity and inclusion officers play a crucial role in fostering an inclusive and culturally competent work environment in today's globalized business landscape. Understanding the Trompenaars'

Cultural Dimensions Framework is essential to navigating the complexities of cultural differences. This subchapter aims to provide diversity and inclusion officers and business professionals focused on intercultural competence with a comprehensive overview of this framework.

Fons Trompenaars, a renowned Dutch author and consultant, developed the Cultural Dimensions Framework to help individuals and organizations understand and manage cultural diversity. This framework has seven dimensions that highlight various cultural orientations and provide insights into how people from different cultures perceive and approach situations. Trompenaars was a prominent figure in the field of cross-cultural communication and management.

The first dimension, Universalism vs. Particularism, examines whether cultures prioritize rules and principles universally or adapt them based on specific circumstances. This dimension is crucial in understanding how individuals from different cultures navigate ethical dilemmas and make decisions.

The second dimension, Individualism vs. Communitarianism, explores the extent to which cultures emphasize individual autonomy versus collective identity.

Understanding this dimension is vital for promoting teamwork and collaboration across diverse cultures. This dimension was similar to Hofstede's dimension.

The third dimension, Neutral vs. Affective, focuses on how cultures express emotions and handle conflicts. Some cultures tend to be more reserved and neutral, while others are more expressive and effective. Recognizing these differences can help avoid misunderstandings and facilitate effective communication. Neutral cultures tend to control and subdue emotional expressions, whereas emotional cultures encourage the display of feelings.

The fourth dimension, Specific vs. Diffuse, refers to the extent to which cultures separate work and personal life. Some cultures maintain clear boundaries, while others integrate personal relationships into professional settings. This dimension is crucial for building and maintaining relationships across cultures.

The fifth dimension, Achievement vs. Ascription (a belief or claim that something is caused by something else), examines how cultures perceive status and success. In some cultures, achievement is based on personal attributes and competencies, while in others, it is attributed to age, gender, or social connections. Recognizing these differences helps us understand how individuals from different cultures strive for success. In achievement-oriented cultures, status is based on one's accomplishments.

The sixth dimension, Sequential vs. Synchronous, focuses on how cultures perceive time. Some cultures value punctuality and adhere strictly to schedules, while others have a more flexible and fluid approach to time management. Understanding this dimension is crucial for effective cross-cultural collaboration. Sequential time cultures view time linearly, focusing on punctuality and schedules. Synchronous time cultures perceive time as a cycle where various tasks can be done simultaneously, and a more flexible approach to time is adopted.

The seventh dimension, Internal vs. External Control, explores how cultures perceive control over their lives. Some cultures believe in personal control and individual responsibility, while others attribute control to external factors such as fate or societal norms. Recognizing these differences helps in understanding motivation and decision-making processes. Cultures with an internal control orientation believe in controlling outcomes and taking charge of their environment.

By understanding and applying Trompenaars' Cultural Dimensions Framework, diversity and inclusion officers can enhance their intercultural competence as business professionals. This framework offers valuable insights into cultural differences, enabling them to develop strategies that promote inclusivity, effective communication, and collaboration across diverse cultures. Additionally, business professionals can leverage this framework to navigate intercultural challenges, foster understanding, and build strong global relationships.

In conclusion, the Trompenaars' Cultural Dimensions Framework provides a roadmap to intercultural competence in business. By embracing the insights offered by this framework, diversity and inclusion officers and business professionals can enhance their ability to navigate cultural differences, foster inclusivity, and ultimately drive business success in today's increasingly interconnected world.

Applying Cultural Dimensions in Business Decision Making

Successful business decision-making requires a deep understanding and appreciation of cultural differences in today's globalized world. The countries associated with both frameworks can be found online. The ability to navigate cultural nuances and adapt strategies accordingly is vital for business professionals. This subchapter aims to provide diversity and inclusion officers and individuals interested in developing their intercultural competence for business with insights and strategies to apply cultural dimensions in decision-making processes.

As introduced by renowned sociologist Geert Hofstede, cultural dimensions represent the various aspects of culture that influence individuals' behavior and values. These dimensions include power distance, individualism vs. collectivism, masculinity vs. femininity, uncertainty avoidance, and long-term vs. short-term orientation. Understanding these dimensions enables professionals to anticipate and address potential challenges arising from cultural differences.

One key aspect of applying cultural dimensions in decision-making is recognizing the impact of power distance. Different cultures have varying levels of acceptance of hierarchical structures and authority. For example, in high power distance cultures, decisions may require approval from top-level executives, while in low power distance cultures, decisions can be made more collaboratively. Awareness of these differences helps professionals adapt their decision-making processes accordingly, ensuring inclusivity and effective communication.

Additionally, individualism vs. collectivism plays a significant role in decision-making. Individualistic cultures prioritize personal goals and achievements, while collectivist cultures focus on group harmony and consensus. Professionals must consider these cultural tendencies when making decisions, ensuring that the perspectives and needs of all stakeholders are taken into account.

Another dimension to consider is uncertainty avoidance. Cultures with high uncertainty avoidance tend to be risk-averse and prefer clear guidelines, while cultures with low uncertainty avoidance are more comfortable with ambiguity and uncertainty. Professionals must adapt decision-making processes to align with the cultural preference for risk-taking or risk-aversion, ensuring that decisions

13

are well- received and implemented. Furthermore, understanding long-term vs. short-term orientation is crucial for effective decision-making in different cultural contexts. Cultures with a long-term orientation prioritize perseverance, thrift, and future planning, while those with a short-term orientation focus on immediate results and gratification. Professionals must consider these cultural tendencies when developing strategies, ensuring they align with cultural values and expectations.

In conclusion, applying cultural dimensions in business decision-making is essential for professionals aiming to navigate the complexities of the global marketplace. By understanding and appreciating cultural differences, diversity and inclusion officers and individuals seeking intercultural competence can make informed decisions that respect and include diverse perspectives. This subchapter serves as a roadmap for professionals to develop their ability to apply cultural dimensions effectively, enabling them to thrive in today's interconnected business environment. Obtaining an Intercultural Development Inventory (IDI) assessment or similar intercultural competence assessments can significantly relate to effectively discerning and acting on Hofstede's and Trompenaars' cultural dimensions frameworks and their alignment with the organization's vision.

3 DEVELOPING SELF-AWARENESS AND CULTURAL INTELLIGENCE

Self-Reflection and Awareness of Cultural Bias

Diversity and inclusion officers are crucial in fostering intercultural competence within organizations in today's globalized world. As businesses expand their operations across borders, it becomes essential for professionals to develop a global mindset and navigate cultural differences effectively. In this context, self-reflection and awareness of cultural bias are vital tools for enhancing intercultural competence.

Self-reflection is a powerful tool that allows individuals to introspect, identify their cultural biases and assumptions, and act! It examines one's beliefs, values, and behaviors and critically analyzes how they might influence interactions with people from different cultures. By self-reflection, business professionals can better understand their cultural lens and recognize any biases that may hinder effective intercultural communication.

Cultural bias refers to the tendency to favor one's culture and interpret other cultures through one's values and beliefs. It is a natural human tendency but can create barriers to intercultural understanding. By acknowledging and addressing cultural biases, professionals can develop a more open-minded and inclusive approach to cross-cultural interactions.

To promote self-reflection and awareness of cultural bias, diversity and inclusion officers can implement various strategies that align with the vision. What does that mean? For example, there is a tendency to start right in and create training programs and workshops organized to encourage participants to critically reflect on their cultural assumptions without regard for the business impact or results.

To be aligned with the vision-- training (learning), or any initiatives for that matter, must be aligned with the organization's values, purpose, and what they do (the mission). This may often not be the case. The organization must ask themselves what that mission looks like three or five years from now (the vision). The mistake some organizations make is to quickly read over the mission and vision and start right in on creating training programs and initiatives. These initiatives might include many activities, discussions, and technology that challenge participants' preconceived notions,

 encourage them to question their biases, and still not be aligned with the vision for business impact. They must go back and read in detail the mission and vision for each element's comprehensive meaning, understanding, and intent and how it can be measured accurately. This is the start of alignment.

Additionally, diversity and inclusion officers can facilitate opportunities for professionals to engage in intercultural experiences. For example, this could include international assignments, cross-cultural projects, virtual exchange programs, or initiatives that might be related to an individual or group intercultural development plan if they have taken the intercultural development inventory and received a development plan. By immersing themselves in different cultural contexts, professionals can gain firsthand exposure to diverse perspectives and enhance their intercultural competence. However, without a structured development plan, immersing oneself in a different culture may not improve one's intercultural competence.

Furthermore, diversity and inclusion officers should encourage ongoing self-reflection and provide resources for professionals to continue their personal development in alignment with measured indicators toward the vision. Some companies do something called an individual scorecard. As previously discussed, resources could include recommended reading materials, online courses, mentorship programs, or assessments. By fostering a culture of continual learning and self-awareness, organizations can ensure that their professionals are ready with the skills necessary to thrive in a globalized business environment in the future.

In conclusion, self-reflection and awareness of cultural bias are essential components of developing intercultural competence in business professionals for impact. Diversity and inclusion officers are crucial in promoting these skills within organizations in collaboration with the business units, HR business partners, and talent development. By encouraging assessment, self-reflection, addressing cultural biases, and providing opportunities for intercultural experiences, organizations can foster a global mindset and enhance their ability to navigate cultural differences for successful business outcomes and impact.

Cultural Intelligence: The Four Components

Organizations must develop intercultural competence among their professionals in today's globalized business environment. This is where the concept of Cultural Intelligence (CQ) can also come into play. The book "The Global Mindset: A Roadmap to Intercultural Competence in Business" discusses four key components of Cultural Intelligence, providing diversity and inclusion officers, as well as business professionals, with a comprehensive understanding of its significance and practical application.

The first component of Cultural Intelligence is cognitive CQ, also known as Cultural Quotient, which refers to one's knowledge and understanding of different cultures. One might also consider this CQ or an individual's knowledge about other cultures. This involves familiarity with cultural norms, values, traditions, and communication styles. Business professionals must educate themselves about cultures to avoid

misunderstandings and effectively collaborate with individuals from diverse backgrounds. Cognitive CQ can be developed through active learning, reading, and cross-cultural experiences.

The second component is metacognitive CQ, what one might call CQ strategy, which focuses on individuals' awareness and control of their own cultural biases and assumptions. Professionals need to recognize their cultural lens and be willing to reflect on their beliefs and behaviors critically. By becoming aware of their cultural biases, business professionals can adapt their approach and become more open-minded and inclusive. A person with a CQ strategy can know and plan for multicultural interactions.

The third component, motivational CQ, or what some might call CQ drive, emphasizes individuals' motivation and confidence in engaging with different cultures. It involves being curious, flexible, and willing to step out of one's comfort zone. Motivational CQ enables professionals to navigate cultural differences with curiosity and adaptability rather than fear or resistance. It encourages a growth mindset that fosters learning and development in intercultural contexts.

The fourth and final component is behavioral CQ, or CQ action, which refers to individuals' ability to adapt their behaviors to different cultural contexts. It involves effectively communicating, building relationships, and resolving conflicts across cultures. Behavioral CQ requires professionals to be sensitive to cultural cues and adjust (take action) their communication style accordingly. This component is crucial for successful cross-cultural collaboration and building strong relationships with clients and colleagues from diverse backgrounds.

By developing all four components of Cultural Intelligence, diversity and inclusion officers can foster intercultural competence among business professionals. This will enable organizations to navigate the complexities of the global market, build strong relationships with clients, and leverage the diverse perspectives and talents of their workforce. This book serves as a valuable resource for understanding and cultivating Cultural Intelligence, providing practical strategies and insights to enhance intercultural competence in the business context; knowledge, drive, strategy, and action in support of, and in alignment with the vision of the organization.

Enhancing Cultural Intelligence in Business Professionals

In today's globalized business landscape, high cultural intelligence (CQ) is crucial for success. As Diversity and Inclusion Officers, you play a pivotal role in fostering an inclusive and culturally competent environment within your organizations. To effectively develop intercultural competence for business professionals, focusing on enhancing their cultural intelligence is essential.

Individuals with cultural intelligence can navigate and work effectively in diverse cultural settings. Its relevance to intercultural competence is the ability to understand and apply the Hofstede and Trompenaars cultural frameworks and use them effectively in real-world situations. It is also relevant to effective cross-cultural interactions, organization development and talent development, training and development, leadership in multicultural settings, and personal and professional growth.

The first step in enhancing cultural intelligence is to provide business professionals with comprehensive cultural knowledge through opportunities for self-assessment and awareness. This includes assessing one's current level of cultural intelligence and intercultural competence. Tools like the Intercultural Development Inventory can be useful to help reflect on one's cultural background, biases, and preconceptions. Recognize how your culture influences your perceptions and interactions.

Educational enrichment, cultural exposure and experiences, developing empathy and open-mindedness, practicing and applying knowledge, reflective practice and continuous learning, seeking feedback and mentorship, implementing aligned organizational strategies, evaluating progress, networking, and collaboration that is culturally diverse. Leadership in these areas that provides insights and integrates learning, leadership, and organizational cultural initiative in a structured approach and comprehensive towards intercultural competence is crucial for today's globalized environment.

Educational enrichment forms the foundation for enhancing Cultural Intelligence, where practitioners are encouraged to expand their knowledge of diverse cultural norms, values, and communication styles. This is complemented by active cultural exposure and experiences, enabling a deeper understanding of different worldviews.

Developing empathy and open-mindedness is critical, as it fosters the ability to view situations through diverse cultural lenses, enhancing interpersonal relationships. Practitioners are advised to actively practice and apply their knowledge in varied contexts, adapting communication and behavior to suit diverse cultural interactions.

Reflective practice and continuous learning are integral to the journey of intercultural competence. This involves regular introspection of intercultural engagements and a commitment to ongoing education in global cultural dynamics. Seeking feedback and mentorship offers valuable external perspectives and guidance, further refining intercultural skills.

Implementing aligned organizational strategies involves integrating cultural intelligence into corporate practices, from diversity training to policy-making. This strategic alignment ensures that the principles of cultural intelligence are not just individual pursuits but are embedded within the organizational culture. Regular evaluation of cultural intelligence and intercultural competence requires leadership to influence organizational outcomes positively, affecting business impact and today's globalized environment.

Cultural skills are crucial for business professionals to engage with individuals from diverse cultural backgrounds effectively. These skills include effective cross-cultural communication, negotiation, conflict resolution, and relationship-building. Providing learning and development programs focusing on developing these skills can significantly enhance professionals' ability to navigate intercultural dynamics and foster successful business relationships.

Lastly, engage in educational activities to expand your knowledge of different cultures. This includes studying cultural norms, values, business practices, and communication styles. Participate in workshops, seminars, or courses on intercultural communication and global diversity. Be flexible, open-minded, and adaptable to new cultural environments. Encourage professionals to step out of their comfort zones, embrace unfamiliar cultural practices, and empower employees to be more agile and responsive in global business settings.

In conclusion, enhancing cultural intelligence is key to developing intercultural competence in business professionals. By focusing on cultural drive, knowledge, strategy, and action, organizations can equip their employees with the necessary skills and tools to navigate the complexities of the global marketplace. As Diversity and Inclusion Officers, your role in promoting cultural intelligence is vital in creating inclusive and culturally competent organizations and the roadmap to thrive in the global business arena.

Assessing and Measuring Cultural Intelligence

In the rapidly evolving global business landscape, diversity and inclusion have become essential components for organizations striving to succeed in international markets. As Diversity and Inclusion Officers, it is crucial to understand and promote intercultural competence among business professionals. This subchapter, "Assessing and Measuring Cultural Intelligence," will provide valuable insights into evaluating and enhancing cultural intelligence within your organization.

Cultural intelligence (CQ) refers to an individual's ability to navigate, adapt, and communicate effectively across different cultures. It goes beyond cultural awareness and sensitivity, encompassing a range of skills and behaviors necessary for successful cross-cultural interactions. Assessing and measuring CQ is vital to identify strengths, areas for improvement, and track progress in developing intercultural competence.

Measuring CQ is vital when discussing the development of a

global mindset and ensuring that intercultural competence aligns with an organization's vision and strategic objectives for impactful business outcomes. It helps establish a baseline alignment with strategic objectives, targeted development programs, track progress and impact, enhance global leadership, and improve decision-making.

The first step in assessing CQ is through self-assessment tools. These tools allow individuals to reflect on their cultural experiences, knowledge, and skills. They provide a comprehensive overview of their strengths and weaknesses, aiding in identifying gaps and opportunities for growth. Self-assessment tools can be used as a benchmark to measure progress over time.

Another approach to measuring CQ is through behavioral assessments. These assessments evaluate individuals' ability to adapt their behavior in diverse cultural contexts. They focus on observable behaviors such as verbal and non-verbal communication, conflict resolution, and decision-making. Behavioral assessments provide valuable insights into an individual's performance in intercultural situations, highlighting areas requiring further development.

Cultural intelligence can be evaluated through cross-cultural simulations and role- plays. These experiences recreate real-life scenarios for individuals to apply their knowledge and skills in a controlled environment. Feedback and reflection help people better understand their strengths and areas for improvement.

It is essential to include 360-degree assessments to ensure a holistic measurement of cultural intelligence. These assessments gather feedback from supervisors, peers, and subordinates to comprehensively view an individual's intercultural competence. This feedback can identify blind spots, provide different perspectives, and facilitate targeted development plans.

Finally, it is crucial to establish clear continuous performance improvement (CPI), evaluation schemes, metrics, and benchmarks to track progress in developing cultural intelligence. The Association for Talent Development CPI model and Kirkpatrick's Four Levels of Evaluation are good best practice schemes for this. These performance metrics can include several indicators derived from the mission's and vision's detailed intent that need to be turned into detailed strategies with performance goals that have clear indicators towards achieving the vision. This process was detailed in the book Total Alignment: Tools and Tactics For Streamlining Your Organization by Riaz and Linda Khadem (2017). By regularly reviewing and analyzing these metrics in the CPI process that includes evaluation, you can measure the effectiveness of your diversity and inclusion initiatives and identify areas that require additional support to align with the vision.

In conclusion, assessing and measuring cultural intelligence is paramount for Diversity and Inclusion Officers seeking to enhance intercultural competence among business professionals (being in alignment). Utilizing self-assessment tools, behavioral assessments, cross-cultural simulations, and 360-degree assessments, you can gain valuable insights into individuals' strengths and areas for improvement. Performance management and individual scorecards need not be separate. By establishing clear metrics and benchmarks, you can track progress and ensure the success of your organization's intercultural competence initiatives.

4 EFFECTIVE COMMUNICATION ACROSS CULTURES

Verbal and Non-Verbal Communication Differences

Effective communication is the cornerstone of success in any business setting, but understanding the nuances of verbal and non-verbal communication becomes even more crucial when it comes to intercultural interactions. In today's globalized world, where diversity is celebrated, and inclusion is prioritized, business professionals must possess a high level of intercultural competence to navigate the complexities of cross-cultural communication.

Verbal communication refers to the use of words, spoken or written, to convey messages. However, the way we use language can vary significantly across cultures. While some cultures prefer direct and explicit communication, others prefer indirect and nuanced expressions. For diversity and inclusion officers, recognizing and adapting to these linguistic differences is critical to fostering effective communication within multicultural teams.

Conversely, non-verbal communication encompasses gestures, facial expressions, body language, and even personal space. These non-verbal cues can carry significant meaning in different cultural contexts. For example, maintaining eye contact may be seen as a sign of respect in some cultures, while in others, it may be considered impolite or confrontational. Even a well-intended attempt at a handshake between a woman and a man may be inappropriate. Instead, parties may close their hands palm-to-palm in front of them or touch their hand to their chest or shoulder area in response to your outreached hand in respect. Awareness of these variations is essential for diversity and inclusion officers as they strive to create an inclusive environment where all employees feel valued and understood.

It is crucial to provide training and resources focusing on verbal and non-verbal communication differences to enhance intercultural competence in business professionals. This can include workshops, seminars, and cultural sensitivity training programs specifically designed to address the challenges of cross-cultural communication.

Furthermore, diversity and inclusion officers should encourage an open and inclusive dialogue within the workplace, although these issues can be quite sensitive. Recall from previous frameworks that some cultures do not approach such topics head on. By fostering an environment where individuals feel comfortable discussing their cultural backgrounds and communication preferences (values), professionals can better understand one another and improve overall communication effectiveness.

In conclusion, verbal and non-verbal communication differences play a significant role in intercultural competence for business professionals. Understanding and adapting to these variations is essential for diversity and inclusion officers who aim to create an inclusive work environment. By providing the necessary training and fostering open dialogue, organizations can easily empower their employees to navigate cross-cultural communication and achieve success in today's globalized business landscape.

Regarding verbal communication in a culturally diverse environment, some individuals, like proficient users, may not have a sufficient grasp of the language to understand cultural nuances, idioms, and contextual usage. Consequently, to be an effective cross-cultural communicator, it is likely best to say what you mean and mean what you say without all the nuances, idioms, and contextual language. This would include proficient user communication styles ranging from direct to indirect and adapting to misunderstandings for positive outcomes, including business terminology.

Overcoming Language Barriers in Business

Language barriers can pose significant challenges in today's globalized business environment. Effective communication becomes paramount for success as companies expand their presence in international markets. This subchapter addresses the importance of overcoming language barriers in business and provides strategies for developing intercultural competence in this context.

Understanding how language barriers can hinder effective communication is crucial for diversity and inclusion officers. These officers play a vital role in fostering an inclusive work environment that values diversity. Acknowledging and addressing language barriers can create a more inclusive workplace where everyone can contribute and thrive.

Intercultural competence is a crucial skill for business professionals operating in a globalized world. It involves understanding and appreciating cultural norms, values, and communication styles. Language is a fundamental aspect of culture, and overcoming language barriers is essential for effective intercultural communication.

Professionals can employ several strategies to overcome language barriers in the business world. Firstly, investing in language training programs can significantly enhance intercultural competence. Offering language courses or hiring interpreters can improve communication and foster understanding between colleagues, clients, and partners from different linguistic backgrounds.

Additionally, using technology can be a valuable tool in overcoming language barriers. Translation apps and software can facilitate real-time translation, making communication more efficient and effective. This allows business professionals to engage in conversations and negotiations without being hindered by language differences.

However, it is crucial to remember that language is more than just words; it encompasses non-verbal cues, gestures, and cultural context. Therefore, developing cultural sensitivity is equally important in overcoming language barriers. Business professionals should invest time in learning about the cultural norms and practices of the individuals they interact with. This knowledge helps in navigating potential misunderstandings and building stronger cross-cultural relationships.

In conclusion, language barriers can pose significant challenges in the global business landscape. However, by investing in language training programs, such as Business English or Common European Framework of Reference, utilizing technology, and developing cultural sensitivity, businesses can overcome these barriers and foster effective intercultural communication. Diversity and inclusion officers are pivotal in promoting intercultural competence and creating an inclusive work environment where language differences are seen as assets rather than obstacles. By embracing linguistic diversity, businesses can tap into new markets, build stronger relationships, and gain a competitive edge in today's global marketplace.

Building Trust and Rapport in Intercultural Communication

In today's globalized business landscape, intercultural competence has become critical for professionals to thrive in diverse work environments. Communicating effectively and building trust and rapport across cultural boundaries is essential for success. This subchapter explores strategies and best practices for developing trust and rapport in intercultural communication. It provides valuable insights for diversity and inclusion officers and business professionals seeking to enhance their intercultural competence.

One of the fundamental aspects of building trust and rapport in intercultural communication is developing cultural self-awareness. Understanding our cultural biases, values, and assumptions allows us to approach interactions with an open mind and avoid misunderstandings. Recognizing and challenging our unconscious biases enables us to build genuine connections with individuals from different cultures.

Active listening is another crucial element in building trust and rapport across cultures. Listening attentively and empathetically to others' perspectives fosters mutual understanding and respect. It is essential to demonstrate respect for cultural differences and avoid making assumptions or judgments based on our cultural norms. We can uncover shared values and experiences by actively listening, leading to more meaningful and authentic connections.

Nonverbal communication also plays a significant role in intercultural communication. Different cultures may have distinct body language, eye contact, and personal space norms. For example, in the U.S., inside 18 inches (about 45 cm) is considered a personal zone. In some cultures, being inside 18 inches is quite normal. African Americans do not like it when others touch their hair unsolicited to feel their braids or afro. Being mindful of these cultural nuances and adapting our nonverbal cues can help establish rapport and trust. Additionally, being aware of potential language barriers and using clear and concise language can facilitate effective communication.

Trust is built over time through consistent actions and integrity. Honoring commitments, being reliable, and following through on promises are crucial in establishing trust-based relationships. Cultural sensitivity and respect for diverse perspectives are essential in fostering an environment where individuals feel valued and included.

Finally, it is vital to approach intercultural communication with curiosity and a willingness to learn. Embracing cultural differences and seeking to understand the perspectives of others can lead to stronger relationships and more effective collaboration. Actively seeking opportunities to engage with different cultures, such as participating in cultural exchange programs or diversity training workshops, can enhance intercultural competence and facilitate building trust and rapport.

In conclusion, building trust and rapport in intercultural communication is vital for professionals in today's globalized business world. Individuals can enhance their intercultural competence and foster meaningful connections across cultures by developing cultural self-awareness, practicing active listening, adapting nonverbal communication, demonstrating integrity, and approaching interactions with curiosity. This subchapter provides valuable insights and strategies for diversity and inclusion officers and business professionals seeking to navigate the complexities of intercultural communication and build trust-based relationships.

Conflict Resolution and Negotiation Styles in Different Cultures

Conflict resolution and negotiation styles can vary significantly across different cultures, making it crucial for business professionals to develop intercultural competence in these areas. In this subchapter, we will explore the various approaches to conflict resolution and negotiation in different cultures and how understanding these styles can enhance business relationships and promote effective communication.

The prevailing negotiation style is often direct and assertive in many Western cultures, such as the United States and Western Europe. Business professionals from these cultures tend to value efficiency, clarity, and getting straight to the point. Conflict resolution strategies may involve open discussion, debate, and reaching a compromise that satisfies both parties' interests.

In contrast, many Asian cultures, such as China and Japan, emphasize harmony and preserving face. I would say this is also true in Malaysia, where I live. Negotiation styles in these cultures often involve indirect communication, nonverbal cues, and a focus on building relationships before discussing business matters. This might involve tea, coffee, or small bite size meals before business is conducted. If you try otherwise, you may be asked if you had your tea or coffee. A hint that it's not time for business yet. Conflict resolution strategies may involve mediation, seeking consensus, and maintaining a harmonious atmosphere.

In the Middle East, cultural norms and traditions can highly influence negotiation styles. Relationships and personal connections play a significant role, and business professionals may engage in extensive small talk and socializing before getting down to business. Conflict resolution may involve the use of intermediaries, such as respected community members or religious leaders, to mediate disputes.

Latin American cultures tend to prioritize personal relationships and trust-building in negotiations. Business professionals may engage in extensive small talk, socializing, and building rapport before discussing business matters. Conflict resolution strategies may involve compromise, collaboration, and finding win-win solutions.

Diversity and inclusion officers must understand these different negotiation and conflict resolution styles. Recognizing and respecting cultural differences can help bridge cultural gaps and facilitate effective communication between diverse teams. This understanding can also help avoid misunderstandings, misinterpretations, and potential conflicts. Do not be surprised in Muslim countries, for there to be whole train cars or women only sections where no men are allowed. I have had personal experience with this in Malaysia. After the train moved, it quickly became apparent that I was in the wrong car and had to wait for the next stop to change cars. It felt quite humiliating, so pay attention when culture is involved!

Diversity and inclusion officers should provide training and resources that focus on cultural awareness and understanding to develop intercultural competence in conflict resolution and negotiation. This is a real thing: to be culturally aware of your surroundings and the culture that you are in. Training on such matters can include workshops, case studies, and real-life examples like the one I shared about the women only train compartment that highlights the nuances of culture, negotiation, and conflict resolution in different cultures.

Organizations can foster a global mindset and enhance their intercultural competence by equipping business professionals with the knowledge and skills to navigate these cultural differences. This will lead to more successful negotiations and conflict resolutions, build stronger relationships, and create a more inclusive and harmonious work environment.

5 ADAPTING TO DIFFERENT BUSINESS ETIQUETTE

Understanding Business Etiquette in Various Cultures

In today's globalized world, businesses increasingly operate in diverse cultural contexts. As diversity and inclusion officers, it is crucial to equip business professionals with the necessary intercultural competence to navigate these diverse settings. One key aspect of intercultural competence is understanding and practicing business etiquette in various cultures.

Business etiquette refers to the customary rules and behaviors that govern professional interactions within a specific culture. It encompasses many practices, including communication styles, greeting customs, dress codes, and gift-giving traditions. By understanding and respecting these cultural norms, business professionals can build trust, establish meaningful connections, and enhance their effectiveness in cross-cultural business interactions.

Other essential nuances about business etiquette include body language, dining etiquette, hierarchy, respect for authority, and building relationships and trust. Being adaptable and flexible, having a spirit of continuous learning, being sensitive, and understanding legal and ethical considerations are essential to business etiquette.

Using case studies and real-world examples that illustrate successful navigation of cultural differences in a business setting as part of continuous can also help.

However, every culture has its own unique set of expectations and practices when it comes to business etiquette. For instance, in some cultures, such as Japan, punctuality is highly valued, and being late for a meeting can be perceived as disrespectful. In contrast, in certain Latin American countries, such as Brazil, a more relaxed approach to time is common, and being a few minutes late may be more acceptable. Understanding these cultural differences is essential to avoid misunderstandings and maintain positive relationships.

Effective communication is another crucial aspect of business etiquette. In some cultures, direct and assertive communication styles are preferred, like in the United States, while in others, a more indirect and harmonious approach is valued. For example, in many Asian cultures, such as China, Korea, and Malaysia, saving face and avoiding confrontation is essential. Business professionals should be

mindful of their communication style, choosing their words carefully and being sensitive to non-verbal cues.

Dress codes also vary across cultures, and what may be considered appropriate business attire in one country may be seen as inappropriate in another. For instance, while formal business attire is expected in Western cultures, certain Middle Eastern countries may have more conservative dress codes that require women to cover their shoulders and wear longer skirts. Understanding and adhering to these dress code expectations is essential to demonstrate respect for local customs and traditions.

Gift-giving is yet another important aspect of business etiquette. In some cultures, such as China and Japan, exchanging gifts is a common practice to show appreciation and build relationships. However, in other cultures, such as the Middle East, gifts may be seen as bribes and should be avoided. It is crucial for business professionals to understand the cultural norms surrounding gift-giving and to exercise discretion when engaging in this practice. Dining etiquette varies greatly across cultures. In many parts of Asia and the Middle East, it is customary to eat with one's hands, typically using the right hand, as the left is traditionally reserved for other purposes and considered unclean for eating. While these cultures often provide utensils for foreigners, it's acceptable to request them if not offered. Additionally, sitting on the floor or on a traditional rug with legs crossed during meals in these regions is typical, rather than at a table with chairs.

In building business relationships and trust, it's crucial to be mindful of cultural and religious norms governing interactions between genders in some countries. For instance, in certain cultures, prolonged eye contact with women, engaging in private conversations (involving just two people), or sharing casual social activities like having coffee, tea, or lunch with a woman in the absence of others might be considered inappropriate or 'haram' (forbidden), primarily if the individuals are not related or married. This extends to physical contact; thus, actions like shaking hands, displaying signs of affection, or holding hands in public are generally uncommon in these settings if the individuals are not related or married. Foreign men, in particular, may be unaware of these cultural norms. In such contexts, a woman might face significant consequences, including being taken into custody. In contrast, the foreign man might face no repercussions or, in some cases, be asked to leave the country. Awareness and respect for these cultural norms are vital for maintaining professional decorum and ensuring mutual respect in business interactions.

In conclusion, understanding business etiquette in various cultures is vital to intercultural competence for business professionals. Professionals can navigate diverse business environments with confidence and respect by familiarizing themselves with the customs and expectations of different cultural contexts. As diversity and inclusion officers, we are responsible for providing the necessary training and resources to develop this crucial skill set, enabling businesses to thrive in an increasingly interconnected world.

Greetings, Introductions, and Handshakes

Effective communication and building strong relationships with people from diverse cultural backgrounds have become essential for success in today's globalized business world. This subchapter will explore the significance of greetings, introductions, and handshakes in intercultural business settings and guide the development of the necessary skills to foster positive connections.

Understanding cultural norms and practices related to greetings is crucial in establishing a favorable first impression. Different cultures have distinct ways of greeting others, ranging from verbal exchanges to physical gestures. For instance, in many Western cultures, a firm handshake (not crushing) while maintaining eye contact is customary to greet someone. However, in Asian cultures, not having a firm handshake is ok, or maybe a gentle bow or a slight nod often accompanies greetings. Muslims may often greet each other by saying, 'As-salamu alaykum' (Assalamualaykum, Assalamualaikum), meaning 'Peace be upon you.' The reply might be something like 'Salam,' or 'Wa alaikum salam,' or variant thereof, meaning 'and peace be upon you.' So, a non-Muslim would not use this language but instead respond with a customary greeting like good morning or afternoon. One reason it would not be appropriate for a non-Muslim to respond to As-salamu alaykum with Wa alaikum salam as it implies that they, too, are also Muslim! People might get the wrong impression. Awareness of these differences is vital to avoid potential misunderstandings and respect cultural diversity.

Introductions are pivotal in intercultural business encounters, setting the tone for further interactions. Introducing oneself and others appropriately, can help create a comfortable environment and build trust. Understanding the cultural importance placed on titles, names, and formalities is essential. In some cultures, using titles or formal language when addressing individuals in professional settings is customary, while in others, using first names is more common. By adapting to these cultural nuances, business professionals can demonstrate their intercultural competence and establish rapport with their counterparts.

34

The subchapter will also highlight the significance of handshakes as a universal symbol of greeting and agreement. Handshakes are not merely physical gestures but also convey essential cultural messages. The strength of a handshake, the duration, and the use of the left or right hand can vary across cultures. Understanding these subtleties is crucial to avoid unintended offense or discomfort. Adapting one's handshake style to match the cultural context is an essential skill for professionals engaging in international business.

This subchapter offered some practical tips and techniques to enhance intercultural competence in greetings, introductions, and handshakes. It also emphasizes the importance of cultural sensitivity, active listening, and observation skills. It has also explored some real-life examples to illustrate the impact of effective greetings, introductions, and handshakes on building solid cross-cultural relationships.

Ultimately, mastering greetings, introductions, and handshakes represents a fundamental step towards cultivating a global mindset and fostering intercultural competence. This foundational knowledge enables business professionals to make positive first impressions and demonstrates respect and appreciation for cultural diversity. By adeptly navigating these initial interactions, professionals pave the way for meaningful connections and trust-building. Such cultural adeptness is critical for successful engagement in diverse business environments and contributes to more effective international collaboration and negotiation. Professionals excel in a globalized business landscape through these nuanced understandings and adaptations.

Business Attire and Appearance

In today's interconnected and diverse business world, the importance of understanding and respecting cultural norms and practices cannot be overstated. This is particularly true when it comes to business attire and appearance, as our clothing choices often communicate a great deal about our professionalism, credibility, and respect for others.

For diversity and inclusion officers and professionals seeking to enhance their intercultural competence in business, understanding the nuances of business attire across different cultures is crucial. In many cultures, business attire is not merely a matter of personal preference but an important symbol of status, authority, and professionalism.

First and foremost, it is essential to recognize that there is no one-size-fits-all approach to business attire. Different cultures have different expectations and norms, so it is important to familiarize oneself with them before engaging in cross-cultural business interactions. For example, while Western business culture often emphasizes formal attire, such as suits and ties for men and tailored dresses or pantsuits for women, other cultures may have different expectations. In some Asian countries, for instance, a more conservative and modest approach to dressing is generally preferred.

Furthermore, understanding the role of color symbolism in different cultures is crucial. Colors can carry significant cultural meanings, and wearing an inappropriate color in a business setting can have unintended consequences. For instance, in some cultures, black is associated with mourning. It may be perceived as inappropriate for a business meeting, while in others, such as China, red is considered auspicious and is often worn to convey good luck and prosperity.

Additionally, grooming and personal hygiene play a vital role in business appearances. Taking care of one's appearance, including neatness, cleanliness, and grooming, is universally valued in business. Attention to detail in grooming can demonstrate respect for oneself and others and contribute to one's overall professionalism and credibility.

In conclusion, this subchapter on Business Attire and Appearance emphasizes the importance of intercultural competence in understanding and navigating diverse business environments. Diversity and inclusion officers and professionals can enhance their effectiveness in cross-cultural interactions by being aware of and respecting cultural norms and practices around business attire and appearance. Ultimately, the goal is to foster mutual understanding, respect, and successful collaborations in today's globalized business landscape.

Business Meetings and Networking Events

In today's globalized business world, navigating and excelling in cross-cultural settings is an essential skill for business professionals. Understanding and leveraging cultural differences in business meetings and networking events can enhance collaboration, increase opportunities, and improve business outcomes. This subchapter explores the importance of intercultural competence in these settings and provides practical strategies for diversity and inclusion officers to foster a global mindset among their business professionals.

Business meetings serve as a platform for individuals from diverse backgrounds to come together and exchange ideas. However, cultural differences in communication styles, decision-making processes, and hierarchy can often hinder effective collaboration. By cultivating intercultural competence, diversity and inclusion officers can help business professionals develop a deep understanding of cultural norms and adapt their communication and decision-making approaches accordingly.

On the other hand, networking events provide unique opportunities to connect with professionals from various cultural backgrounds and build valuable relationships. However, cultural nuances in networking etiquette, body language, and conversation topics can influence the success of these interactions. Diversity and inclusion officers can enhance their networking effectiveness and foster meaningful connections across cultures by equipping business professionals with the necessary skills to navigate these cultural differences.

To develop intercultural competence in business professionals, diversity and inclusion officers can implement a range of strategies. These include providing cultural awareness training, organizing cross-cultural team-building activities, and offering mentorship programs that pair individuals with diverse backgrounds. Additionally, promoting cultural intelligence and fostering an inclusive work environment that celebrates diversity can further enhance the intercultural competence of business professionals.

Networking events offer a rich tapestry of opportunities for professionals to engage with diverse cultural backgrounds, fostering a global mindset crucial in today's interconnected business world. While these events are invaluable for building valuable relationships, they also present unique challenges due to varying cultural norms in networking etiquette, body language, and appropriate conversation topics. Missteps in these areas, albeit unintentional, can lead to misunderstandings or missed connections. Therefore, equipping business professionals with the skills to navigate these cultural differences adeptly is imperative. Diversity and inclusion officers play a key role in offering training and guidance to enhance intercultural communication skills. Such preparation not only enhances networking effectiveness but also ensures that these interactions contribute to broader organizational goals of global collaboration and success. In cultivating these skills, professionals can more effectively bridge cultural gaps, leading to more fruitful relationships and synergistic partnerships that drive business success in a global context.

In conclusion, business meetings and networking events are crucial in today's global business landscape. Diversity and inclusion officers can empower business professionals with the necessary skills to excel in cross-cultural interactions by addressing the specific challenges posed by cultural differences in these settings. By focusing on intercultural competence, organizations can foster a global mindset, enhance collaboration, and drive success in the increasingly diverse and interconnected business world.

6 BUILDING GLOBAL TEAMS AND COLLABORATION

Strategies for Building and Managing Diverse Teams

Diversity has emerged as a critical component of success in today's globalized business landscape. Companies across industries are realizing the immense benefits of building and managing diverse teams. By harnessing the power of different perspectives, cultures, and experiences, organizations can drive innovation and creativity and, ultimately, achieve better business outcomes. However, effectively building and managing diverse teams requires a strategic approach beyond tokenism or a checkbox exercise. This subchapter explores essential strategies for diversity and inclusion officers and business professionals to enhance their intercultural competence and successfully navigate the challenges and opportunities of diverse teams.

1. Creating an Inclusive Culture: Foster an inclusive culture that values and respects each team member's unique contributions. Encourage open dialogue, active listening, and empathy to ensure everyone feels heard and included.

2. Recruitment and Hiring Practices: Implement unbiased recruitment and hiring practices that attract diverse talent pools. Rethink traditional job descriptions and roles, use diverse sourcing strategies to include skills-based, and establish partnerships with organizations that focus on underrepresented groups.

3. Cultural Competence Training: Provide intercultural competence assessment and training to employees at all levels, enabling them to understand and appreciate different cultural norms, communication styles, and perspectives. Such training enhances empathy, reduces bias, and promotes effective collaboration. Contact your Intercultural Development Inventory Qualified Assessor today and get started!

4. Team Building Activities: Engage in activities that foster trust, collaboration, and understanding among team members. Encourage individuals to share their cultural backgrounds, experiences, and values to build a sense of belonging and create a strong team bond. Activities that can enhance the dynamics of a diverse team might be cultural exchange workshops, skill-sharing sessions, international cuisine days, cross-cultural team projects, global virtual teams, language exchanges, celebrating cultural festivals, professional development workshops, team retreats, feedback and reflection sessions, mentoring and buddy systems, and community service projects.

5. Communication and Language: Promote effective cross-cultural communication by addressing and overcoming language barriers. To be a more effective communicator, encourage using plain language, avoid jargon, and provide resources for language support where necessary.

6. Conflict Resolution: Develop conflict resolution strategies that acknowledge and respect cultural differences. Encourage open dialogue and mediation to promote understanding and find mutually

beneficial solutions. The Common European Framework of Reference for Languages (CEFR) proficiency objectives and can-do statements can be used to help create curriculums and lesson plans for this.

7. Leadership Support: It is crucial for organizational leaders to actively support and champion diversity and inclusion strategic initiatives as a cornerstone of fostering a global mindset aligned with the vision. This involves leaders not just endorsing these efforts but being proactive role models. They should consistently demonstrate inclusive behaviors in their daily interactions and decision-making processes. Regularly communicating the importance of diversity in a global context and its alignment with the organization's vision is key; a handwritten, focused feedback about the values read at the top of a meeting works! Leaders should also hold themselves and their teams accountable for fostering an environment where diverse perspectives are respected and actively sought and integrated into business strategies. This ensures that diversity and inclusion are not peripheral concerns but central to the organization's culture and global success.

8. Continuous Evaluation and Improvement: Regularly assess team dynamics, identify areas for improvement, and adapt strategies accordingly. Encourage team feedback and implement necessary changes to optimize diversity and inclusion efforts. As part of strategic alignment, mapping, skills-based metrics, individual scorecards, and performance management can be effective.

The role of leadership in actively cultivating a global mindset through practical actions and strategic alignment and making diversity and inclusion integral to organizational success cannot be over emphasized. By adopting these strategies, diversity and inclusion officers and business professionals can cultivate an intercultural competence that will maximize the potential of diverse teams. Embracing diversity is not just a moral imperative but a strategic advantage that positions organizations for success in an increasingly interconnected world.

Leveraging Diversity for Innovation and Creativity

In an era marked by unprecedented global interconnectedness, harnessing diversity and inclusion is a key differentiator in driving business innovation. This subchapter delves into how embracing and leveraging the richness of diverse views, backgrounds, and experiences can ignite a powerful force for creative thinking and innovative problem-solving. We explore practical strategies for transforming the workplace into a dynamic incubator for novel ideas and breakthrough solutions, demonstrating that when diversity is effectively leveraged, it is more than a social imperative— it is a catalyst for business excellence and competitive advantage.

Diversity goes beyond just gender, race, or ethnicity. It encompasses different perspectives, experiences, and cultural backgrounds. By embracing diversity, organizations can tap into a wealth of varied knowledge, skills, and ideas. This diversity of thought can lead to breakthrough innovations and creative solutions that can give companies a competitive edge and help achieve their strategic objectives.

One of the key benefits of diversity is the ability to bring together individuals with different ways of thinking. When people from diverse backgrounds collaborate and are allowed to express themselves, they bring unique insights and alternative perspectives to the table. This intercultural exchange of ideas sparks creativity and encourages innovative thinking and solutions by challenging the status quo.

Moreover, diversity fosters a culture of inclusion and psychological safety, where employees feel valued and empowered to contribute their ideas. When individuals feel comfortable expressing their opinions without fear of judgment or discrimination, it creates an environment that nurtures creativity and innovation. By creating an inclusive workplace, organizations can inspire employees to think outside the box and take calculated risks. It can also help improve employee engagement!

Research consistently shows a positive correlation between diversity, innovation, and profits. Studies have found that diverse teams outperform homogeneous teams in problem-solving, decision-making, and generating novel ideas. By leveraging diversity, companies can access broader perspectives, cultural insights, and problem-solving approaches, leading to more innovative and successful outcomes aligned with the vision.

However, leveraging diversity for innovation and creativity requires more than just having a diverse workforce. It requires fostering a culture that embraces diverse perspectives, encourages collaboration, and values open-mindedness. This is a full circle moment back to a consensus and detailed understanding of the intent of the mission's specific elements and what that looks like three to five years from now, the vision. This, too, must have a detailed and measurable understanding of its intent. Diversity and inclusion officers promote diversity training, drive this cultural transformation, and facilitate cross-cultural collaboration.

In conclusion, leveraging diversity for innovation and creativity is crucial in today's globalized business environment. By embracing diversity and creating an inclusive workplace, organizations can tap into the vast potential of diverse perspectives, experiences, and cultures. This subchapter serves as a guide for diversity and inclusion officers and business professionals interested in assessing and developing their intercultural competence and harnessing the power of diversity to drive innovation and creativity within their organizations.

Virtual Collaboration and Cross-Cultural Communication Technologies

In today's digitally connected era, the landscape of global business necessitates seamless virtual collaboration, bringing together teams and clients from varied cultural backgrounds. As diversity and inclusion officers, comprehending the intricacies of virtual collaboration and cross-cultural communication technologies is paramount. These technologies are pivotal in cultivating intercultural competence among business professionals. This subchapter delves into the critical aspects and strategies surrounding these tools, emphasizing their role in nurturing a global mindset.

Virtual collaboration involves leveraging digital platforms such as Zoom, Microsoft Teams, Slack, and Asana, which enable individuals and teams from different corners of the world to collaborate effectively. These tools facilitate communication and project management and bridge cultural and geographical divides, allowing businesses to harness a wide range of talent and diverse perspectives. However, this collaboration mode comes with its own challenges, especially in cross-cultural communication. Differences in time zones, cultural communication styles, and technology familiarity can impact the dynamics of virtual teamwork. Understanding and navigating these challenges is crucial for maximizing the benefits of virtual collaboration and ensuring effective, culturally sensitive communication across global teams.

Cross-cultural communication technologies, encompassing video conferencing, instant messaging, project management software, and virtual reality tools, are more than just facilitators of global connectivity; they are strategic assets in an organization's quest to achieve its vision and business objectives. By adeptly leveraging these technologies, business professionals can surmount common hurdles of international collaboration, such as language barriers, time zone differences, and diverse cultural norms, thereby enhancing communication effectiveness.

The strategic value of these technologies lies in their ability to foster more cohesive and efficient global teams, leading to several key organizational benefits:

1. **Improved Collaboration and Productivity**: Seamless communication tools enable teams spread across various geographies to collaborate in real time, improving project turnaround times and overall productivity.

2. **Enhanced Innovation**: Diverse perspectives are a wellspring of innovation. When teams communicate effectively across cultural boundaries, they are more likely to generate innovative solutions to complex problems.

3. **Expanded Global Reach**: These technologies facilitate more accessible entry into new markets by enhancing communication with local partners and understanding regional market dynamics.

4. **Increased Employee Engagement and Retention**: Employees who feel connected and valued in a global team are more likely to be engaged and committed to the organization, reducing turnover rates.

5. **Cost Efficiency**: Virtual collaboration tools can significantly reduce travel and operational costs, allowing for more efficient allocation of resources.

6. **Risk Mitigation**: Effective communication across cultures minimizes misunderstandings and potential conflicts, reducing the risk of costly errors or delays in project completion.

Another key benefit of virtual collaboration and cross-cultural communication technologies is their opportunity for intercultural competence development. Intercultural competence is the ability to effectively interact and communicate with individuals from different cultural backgrounds for positive outcomes (essential). These technologies allow professionals to engage in virtual meetings, brainstorming sessions, and collaborative projects that facilitate cultural exchange, understanding, and completing development plans.

Moreover, these technologies enable participants to experience virtual immersion in different cultural contexts. For instance, virtual reality tools can simulate real-world scenarios, allowing individuals to gain firsthand exposure to different cultural perspectives. Such experiences enhance empathy, cultural sensitivity, and the ability to adapt to diverse business environments aligned with the vision.

To maximize the effectiveness of virtual collaboration and cross-cultural communication technologies, diversity and inclusion officers must provide intercultural competence assessment, training and support to business professionals. This may include continued counseling for intercultural development plans, workshops on intercultural communication, virtual collaboration best practices, and the effective use of communication technologies. Additionally, it is essential to create a culture of inclusivity and respect within the organization, where diverse perspectives are valued and encouraged.

In conclusion, the strategic deployment of cross-cultural communication technologies directly aligns with and supports an organization's vision and strategic objectives essential for fostering intercultural competence among business professionals. Some sample performance goals might include improvements in global team collaboration efficiency, employee engagement in multicultural environments, reduction in cultural miscommunication incidents, expansion of global market reach, language barrier reduction, and increase in cross-cultural training participation. By leveraging these technologies and setting goals, professionals can break down cultural barriers, enhance communication effectiveness, and develop a global mindset. As diversity and inclusion officers, we are responsible for promoting the adoption and effective use of these technologies. They are not just tools for bridging the cultural divide but pivotal elements in driving business success, global expansion, and competitive advantage in today's interconnected business world.

Addressing Challenges in Global Teamwork

In today's interconnected world, businesses are increasingly operating on a global scale, which has led to the rise of global teams. These teams bring together individuals from diverse cultural backgrounds, each with their own unique perspectives and ways of working. While global teamwork offers immense opportunities for innovation and growth, it also presents its fair share of challenges. This subchapter delves into the various hurdles that diversity and inclusion officers, as well as professionals seeking intercultural competence in business, may encounter in managing and working within global teams.

One of the primary challenges in global teamwork is communication. Effective communication has been mentioned before but is worth repeating here and is vital for collaboration, knowledge sharing, and decision-making. However, language barriers, different communication styles, and cultural norms can hinder effective communication within global teams. The subchapter explores strategies for overcoming these challenges, such as providing language training, encouraging open dialogue, and promoting active listening.

Another key challenge is managing conflict within global teams. This is a big one as mentioned previously during the sections on Hofstede's and Trompenaar's cultural dimensions! Cultural differences can lead to misunderstandings and disagreements, which, if not addressed appropriately, can escalate and impact team dynamics. This subchapter provides insights on conflict resolution techniques that embrace cultural diversity, encouraging individuals to empathize with one another's perspectives and find common ground. Here are some summary objectives **derived** from the supplementary descriptors from Appendix 8 of the CEFR Companion volume. For specific and exact objectives, please refer to the CEFR and Association of Language Testers in Europe can do statements:

1. **Understanding Cultural Nuances in Communication (B2-C1 Level)**: Can understand the main ideas of complex text on both concrete and abstract topics, including technical discussions in their field of specialization, recognizing implicit cultural meanings.

2. **Expressing and Interpreting Emotions and Opinions (B2-C1 Level)**: Can interact with a degree of fluency and spontaneity that makes regular interaction with native speakers quite possible without strain for either party, acknowledging and respecting cultural differences in expression.

3. **Negotiating and Persuading in a Culturally Sensitive Manner (C1 Level)**: Can express themselves fluently and convey finer shades of meaning precisely, negotiating and persuading effectively in a culturally sensitive manner and conducive to finding common ground.

4. **Dealing with Conflict in Diverse Teams (B2-C2 Level)**: Can identify the source of conflict in an intercultural context and propose effective solutions, mediating between parties with cultural sensitivity and aiming for mutually beneficial outcomes.

5. **Adapting Language According to the Audience (B2-C2 Level)**: Can adapt their language and behavior in a culturally appropriate way, using strategies such as paraphrasing, summarizing, and non-verbal communication to ensure clarity and reduce misunderstandings.

Such objectives can be the basis for focused outcomes and training content. The actual can do statements and descriptors in these documents are quite extensive, and readers are encouraged to view them for yourselves: CEFR supplemental companion volume and Association of Language Testers in Europe.

Building trust and effective leadership are pivotal in global teamwork. Trust, often challenged by cultural differences and geographical distances, forms the cornerstone of successful collaboration. This subchapter offers insights into fostering trust, emphasizing the need for leaders in global teams to possess intercultural competence, adaptability, and cultural understanding. I am, lastly, advocating for leadership styles that promote inclusivity and harness the strengths of diversity.

In conclusion, global teamwork embodies a mix of opportunities and challenges. This section aims to provide diversity and inclusion officers and professionals striving for intercultural competence with practical strategies to navigate these complexities.

7 CROSS-CULTURAL LEADERSHIP AND MANAGEMENT

Cultural Differences in Leadership Styles

Understanding and navigating cultural differences is crucial for success in today's globalized business world. One area where these differences become particularly evident is in leadership styles. Different cultures have distinct approaches to leadership, and being aware of these differences can help diversity and inclusion officers and professionals develop intercultural competence in the business realm.

One key aspect of cultural differences in leadership styles is the balance between individualism and collectivism. Individualism is highly valued in Western cultures, such as the United States. Leaders often adopt a transformational style, encouraging innovation and individual responsibility. For example, American leaders like Steve Jobs were known for their visionary approach, motivating individuals to achieve remarkable personal accomplishments and independence in decision-making.

In contrast, collectivist cultures, particularly in many Asian countries, prioritize group harmony and cooperation. A notable example is the Japanese leadership style, often characterized by consensus-building, where decisions are made collectively, and maintaining harmony within the team is paramount. This can be seen in practices like 'nemawashi', a Japanese decision-making approach involving informal, behind-the-scenes consensus-building before formal meetings.

In high-context cultures, such as Japan or China, communication is often nuanced and layered with meaning that extends beyond words. In these cultures, leaders tend to rely on indirect communication, where much of the message is conveyed through nonverbal cues, tone of voice, and conversation context. For instance, a Japanese leader might use 'honne' and 'tatemae', terms that describe the contrast between a person's true feelings and desires ('honne') and the behavior and opinions one displays in public ('tatemae'). This indirect communication style requires a deep understanding of social hierarchy and reading between the lines.

Conversely, in low-context cultures like the United States and Germany, communication tends to be more direct and explicit. Leaders in these cultures often value clear, straightforward instructions and open dialogue. For example, American leaders might adopt a no-nonsense approach to communication, where transparency and clarity are prioritized. Similarly, German leadership often reflects 'Sachlichkeit,' which implies a focus on facts, directness, and objectivity in communication.

Power distance is another critical aspect of cultural differences in leadership styles. Integrating intercultural competence into understanding power distance can transform the approach to leadership styles. In high power distance cultures like Latin America or the Middle East, recognizing the value of authority and clear decision-making is key. However, an interculturally competent leader also seeks to understand subordinates' perspectives, even if the culture doesn't traditionally encourage it. Conversely, in low power distance cultures such as Scandinavian countries, while participatory decision-making is the norm, an effective leader also appreciates the need for decisive leadership when necessary. Thus, intercultural competence involves balancing cultural expectations with effective leadership practices, adapting to the cultural context while challenging traditional norms where beneficial.

Understanding and appreciating these cultural differences in leadership styles is essential for diversity and inclusion officers and intercultural competence in business professionals. By recognizing and adapting to different leadership approaches, professionals can foster effective collaboration, enhance communication, and build strong relationships with colleagues from diverse cultural backgrounds.

Professionals can engage in cross-cultural training programs to develop intercultural competence, which provides insights into different leadership styles, communication patterns, and cultural norms. Such training can help individuals become more adaptable and sensitive to diverse leadership approaches, enabling them to navigate multicultural environments successfully. Other methods professionals can use to help enhance their leadership and management might be experiential learning, engaging in international assignments and projects, and cultural immersion living in different countries. Mentoring and coaching, networking, self-study, language learning, feedback, and reflection on cross-cultural interactions are more ways for professionals to improve skills in leadership and management.

In conclusion, aligning cultural differences in leadership styles with a business's vision and impact involves recognizing how these differences can influence organizational effectiveness and ROI. Understanding and adapting to these styles can lead to more cohesive, motivated, and productive global teams, directly contributing to business success. For example, intercultural competence can reduce misunderstandings and conflicts, improving efficiency and decision-making. It can also open up new markets and enhance customer relations in different cultural contexts, increasing revenue and market share. Some of these metrics and goals were discussed earlier. Thus, developing intercultural competence is not just about bridging cultural gaps; it's a strategic investment that can yield significant returns by enhancing global business operations and relationships.

Leading and Motivating Multicultural Teams

In today's globalized world, leading and motivating multicultural teams has become an essential skill for business professionals. As diversity and inclusion officers, your role is pivotal in ensuring that organizations embrace and leverage the strengths of multicultural teams. This subchapter aims to provide you with the necessary insights and strategies to foster intercultural competence within your teams, enabling them to thrive in a diverse environment.

First and foremost, it is crucial to understand that multicultural teams bring together individuals with diverse backgrounds, perspectives, and communication styles. Recognizing and valuing these differences and embracing them are the foundations of effective leadership. Encourage an inclusive environment where team members feel safe to express their ideas, opinions, and concerns. Foster open dialogue and active listening, allowing for the exchange and integration of diverse viewpoints for mutual benefits, leading to innovation and better decision-making.

Building cultural intelligence among team members is a key aspect discussed in previous chapters. Cultural intelligence refers to adapting and working effectively in diverse cultural contexts. Encourage team members to develop their cultural knowledge, awareness, and sensitivity. This can be achieved through assessments and cross-cultural training programs, workshops, or simply by creating opportunities for team members to interact and learn from each other's cultures.

To successfully motivate multicultural teams, it is important to understand the diverse motivational factors that drive individuals from different cultural backgrounds. While some may be motivated by individual recognition, others may value collective accomplishments or work-life balance. Tailor your motivational approaches to accommodate these differences, ensuring each team member feels valued and understood. Some of these motivations, hopes, and dreams of individuals can be revealed during regular reviews of individual and team scorecards and performance.

Furthermore, effective leadership in multicultural teams involves managing conflicts arising from cultural differences. This was also discussed in the section on can do statements and cultural interactions for mutual benefits. Conflict resolution techniques that promote understanding and compromise should be encouraged.

Encourage team members to approach conflicts with an open mind, focusing on finding mutually beneficial solutions rather than personal victories.

Lastly, as diversity and inclusion officers, it is essential to lead by example. Embrace diversity yourself and demonstrate inclusive behaviors in your interactions with team members, including the C-Suite, business unit heads, HR business partners, and talent development. If you come to them with solutions aligned with the vision and strategic objectives with business impact, you will likely have their attention. Encourage diversity in recruitment and hiring practices, ensuring that your team reflects the multicultural nature of the business environment aligned with the vision.

Adapting Management Practices to Different Cultures

In today's globalized and competitive business landscape, the ability to navigate (be agile) and succeed in diverse cultural contexts is essential for organizations aiming to thrive in international markets; your vision. As diversity and inclusion officers, your role is pivotal in fostering intercultural competence within your organization and ensuring that management practices are effectively adapted to different cultures. As mentioned before, working closely with the business units, HR business partners, and talent development is key. You must be part of the chain of evidence and alignment for impact. This subchapter aims to provide you with insights and strategies to enhance intercultural competence for business professionals.

Understanding cultural nuances is the first step towards successfully adapting management practices. Each culture has its own unique values, beliefs, and norms that shape how individuals perceive and respond to various managerial approaches. Change management aside, by recognizing these differences, businesses can avoid cultural misunderstandings and develop more effective management strategies. For example, in some cultures, a hierarchical leadership style is valued, while in others, a more participative and collaborative approach is preferred. Such preferences are crucial when managing multicultural teams or conducting business negotiations. For example, Malaysia might be considered an Asian culture that believes in hierarchical leadership, loyalty, and family above imported talent.

Furthermore, it is important to acknowledge that cultural diversity extends beyond national boundaries. A single country can have significant cultural variations based on factors such as ethnicity, religion, and socioeconomic background. By appreciating the complexity of cultural diversity, organizations can create inclusive environments that value and leverage their employees' unique perspectives and contributions. Ignore this at your own peril!

To enhance intercultural competence, organizations should invest in qualified assessments, intercultural development plans, counseling, and training programs that provide business professionals with the necessary skills and knowledge to navigate cultural differences effectively. These programs can include intercultural communication training and strategies, cross-cultural leadership development, and cultural immersion experiences. By equipping employees with the tools to understand, respect, and adapt to different cultures, organizations can foster a global mindset and enhance their ability to compete in international markets.

In addition to training, it is essential to establish organizational structures and policies that support intercultural competence. This starts with a clear and focused understanding of the mission and vision and can include promoting diversity in leadership positions, creating multicultural teams, and encouraging cross-cultural collaboration. By embedding intercultural competence into the fabric of the organization, diversity and inclusion officers can help ensure that management practices are adapted to different cultures and promote a culture of inclusivity.

In conclusion, adapting management practices to different cultures-- better yet, in line with the strategic objectives, is a critical aspect of global business success. By understanding cultural nuances and the values of the organization enshrined in the mission, investing in learning and training programs, and establishing supportive organizational structures, businesses can enhance their intercultural competence and effectively navigate diverse cultural contexts. As diversity and inclusion officers, your role in promoting intercultural competence for business professionals is instrumental in creating inclusive and globally-minded organizations.

Developing Global Managers with Intercultural Competence

In today's interconnected world, effectively navigating cultural differences is crucial for business professionals. As diversity and inclusion officers, you play a pivotal role in fostering an inclusive environment that values and leverages the benefits of cultural diversity. One key aspect of this is developing global managers with intercultural competence. Some examples of action in navigating these differences might be cultural sensitivity training, mentoring and coaching programs, diverse team formation, inclusive leadership development, and employee resource groups.

Recall that intercultural competence refers to understanding, appreciating, and effectively interacting with people from different cultural backgrounds. It goes beyond simply being tolerant or respectful (open-minded); it involves a deep understanding (cognitive) of cultural nuances, the ability to adapt (to act) communication styles, and the capacity to navigate (behavior) diverse work environments.

It is essential to provide them with the necessary knowledge and skills to cultivate global managers with intercultural competence. Some organizations still rely on role-based skills mapping. At the same time, others have already transitioned to skills-based strategy mapping that allows organization-wide flexibility and answers some attrition and future-ready concerns. This can be achieved through comprehensive initiatives and programs that address various aspects of intercultural competence.

Firstly, educating managers about different cultures, including their values, customs, and communication styles, is essential. As most people do not believe there is a problem, it might be best to assess intercultural competence as what gets measured gets done. Some say what gets measured gets management as well. Knowledge of what was evaluated enables them to deeply reflect and potentially develop a global mindset and approach business challenges from a broader perspective. By understanding the unique characteristics of different cultures and where they stand, managers can adapt their leadership styles, decision-making processes, and negotiation techniques to better resonate with diverse teams and clients.

Secondly, effective cross-cultural communication is crucial for global managers. They must be skilled in navigating language barriers, non-verbal cues, and communication styles that vary across cultures. Training on active listening, empathy, and effective verbal and written communication can significantly enhance managers' ability to build strong relationships and collaborate across cultural boundaries.

Thirdly, fostering an appreciation for diversity and inclusion is essential. Managers should understand the benefits of diverse teams and learn how to create an inclusive work environment where everyone feels valued and heard. This involves promoting cultural sensitivity and addressing biases and stereotypes that may hinder effective collaboration.

Lastly, experiential learning opportunities such as international assignments, cultural immersion programs, or virtual collaborations can provide managers with firsthand experience in working across cultures. These experiences help them develop a deeper understanding of different cultural contexts and enhance their ability to adapt, thrive in diverse settings, and improve on their intercultural competence.

Developing global managers with intercultural competence is a continuous process that requires ongoing support and reinforcement. A continuous performance improvement, assessment, and evaluation scheme is required. By investing in their development, organizations can unlock the potential of their diverse workforce, foster innovation, and gain a competitive edge in the global marketplace.

As diversity and inclusion officers, your role in championing intercultural competence is paramount. By advocating for the importance of developing global managers with intercultural competence and implementing comprehensive assessment and training programs, you can contribute to creating a more inclusive and successful business environment aligned with the strategic objectives and vision for business impact.

8 NAVIGATING INTERCULTURAL CHALLENGES IN INTERNATIONAL BUSINESS

Cultural Sensitivity in Marketing and Advertising

In today's interconnected world, cultural sensitivity plays a vital role in the success of marketing and advertising campaigns. As businesses increasingly target diverse markets, professionals must develop a global mindset and embrace intercultural competence. This subchapter explores the significance of cultural sensitivity in marketing and advertising, providing insights and strategies for diversity and inclusion officers and business professionals seeking to enhance their intercultural competence.

Understanding the nuances of different cultures is crucial to developing effective marketing and advertising materials. A lack of cultural sensitivity can lead to miscommunication, misunderstandings, and even offense, damaging a brand's reputation and hindering its success in foreign markets. By recognizing and respecting cultural differences, companies can tailor their messages and visuals to resonate with diverse audiences, driving engagement and brand loyalty.

Diversity and inclusion officers must prioritize research and understanding to achieve cultural sensitivity in marketing and advertising. This involves conducting an in-depth market analysis, considering cultural values, traditions, beliefs, and norms prevalent in the target market. By gaining insights into the target audience's preferences, decision-making processes, and communication styles, businesses can create culturally relevant content that connects with consumers on a deeper level.

Moreover, it is essential to engage local experts and cultural consultants who deeply understand the target market. These professionals can provide invaluable insights into cultural nuances, helping businesses navigate potential pitfalls and ensure their marketing and advertising efforts are culturally appropriate. Collaboration with local partners demonstrates respect for the target culture and strengthens brand credibility and authenticity.

Another crucial aspect of cultural sensitivity in marketing and advertising is avoiding stereotypes and cultural appropriation. Diversity and inclusion officers should encourage creative teams to embrace diversity in their campaigns while avoiding clichés and misrepresentations. By accurately portraying diverse cultures, businesses can resonate with consumers and foster an inclusive brand image.

Furthermore, businesses should be aware of potential language barriers and adapt their messaging accordingly. Translating content accurately is essential, but it is equally important to consider cultural idioms, colloquialisms, and wordplay, as they may not always translate well. Utilizing native speakers and conducting thorough linguistic reviews can help ensure that marketing and advertising materials are culturally sensitive and resonate with the target audience.

In conclusion, cultural sensitivity is a critical factor in the success of marketing and advertising campaigns in today's diverse global marketplace. By embracing intercultural competence and understanding the intricacies of different cultures, businesses can develop content that resonates with diverse audiences, driving engagement and brand loyalty. Diversity and inclusion officers and business professionals seeking to enhance their intercultural competence should prioritize research, deep reflection, collaboration with local experts, and avoiding stereotypes and cultural appropriation. By doing so, they can build inclusive and culturally sensitive marketing and advertising strategies that effectively connect with target markets worldwide.

Understanding Local Laws and Customs in Foreign Markets

In today's globalized world, businesses are increasingly expanding their operations into foreign markets. However, this expansion has numerous challenges, particularly when navigating the complex web of local laws and customs. Business professionals must develop a deep understanding of their legal and cultural landscape to succeed in these markets. This subchapter aims to provide diversity and inclusion officers and professionals interested in intercultural competence for business with a comprehensive roadmap to understanding local laws and customs in foreign markets.

First and foremost, understanding local laws is essential for any business looking to establish a presence abroad. Each country has its own legal framework that governs business operations, including regulations on taxation, employment, intellectual property, and import/export procedures. Failure to comply with these laws can result in significant financial and reputational damage. This subchapter will explore various legal considerations, including the importance of seeking legal counsel, conducting due diligence, and staying up to date with changes in legislation.

It is crucial to recognize that local laws and customs are not static; they evolve over time. Ongoing education and continuous learning are vital for professionals seeking resources and strategies to stay informed about regulations and customs changes, including networking with local professionals, attending cultural training programs, and engaging with local communities. To gain insights into local laws and customs in foreign markets, several online resources can be valuable:

1. The International Trade Administration (ITA) - Foreign Regulations: This platform provides comprehensive information on foreign import regulations, documentation requirements, product standards, and tariffs. It is particularly useful for understanding the legal requirements for exporting to different markets. The ITA also offers resources on resolving trade problems and protecting intellectual property. For more information, ITA - Foreign Regulations.

2. ITA - International Market Research: This section helps businesses research foreign markets, providing access to country reports, market conditions, opportunities, regulations, and customs. It is a crucial resource for conducting due diligence and identifying potential markets. Explore more at ITA - International Market Research.

3. Country Commercial Guides: Prepared by U.S. Embassies worldwide, these guides offer detailed reports on market conditions, opportunities, regulations, and business customs for various countries. They are a valuable tool for businesses looking to understand a target market's specific legal and cultural landscape. Find these guides at Country Commercial Guides.

In conclusion, these resources provide a starting point for professionals and diversity and inclusion officers interested in developing a comprehensive understanding of local laws and customs in foreign markets. They are instrumental in helping businesses navigate the complexities of global expansion and align their strategies with local legal and cultural norms. By equipping diversity and inclusion officers, as well as business professionals interested in intercultural competence, with the knowledge and tools to navigate these complexities, this subchapter aims to contribute to the development of a global mindset necessary for thriving in today's interconnected world and aligned with the vision of the organization.

Managing Ethical Dilemmas in Cross-Cultural Business

Businesses are increasingly operating in diverse cultural contexts in today's interconnected world. This brings with it numerous opportunities but also a range of ethical challenges. As diversity and inclusion officers, it is crucial to understand and navigate these ethical dilemmas to foster a truly inclusive and culturally competent business environment. This subchapter will explore strategies for effectively managing ethical dilemmas in cross-cultural business settings.

One of the key challenges in cross-cultural business is the varying ethical frameworks and values across different cultures. What may be considered acceptable behavior in one culture may be perceived as unethical in another. Therefore, diversity and inclusion officers must develop intercultural competence and sensitivity to navigate these complexities.

To effectively manage ethical dilemmas, it is essential to establish clear ethical guidelines and standards that align with the organization's values. These guidelines should be communicated to all employees, ensuring a shared understanding of ethical expectations. Moreover, these standards should be adaptable and sensitive to cultural nuances while upholding universal ethical principles. One consideration in building an ethical framework and guide is from a business, ethics, and society article, UVA Darden, ideas to action. It talks about clarifying what you know, understanding standards of conduct, clarifying consequences, avoiding rationalizations, and understanding character and virtue. In avoiding rationalizations, the article talks about passing the publicity test, among other assumptions.

A crucial aspect of managing ethics is fostering open communication and dialogue, including organizational risk assessment. Encouraging employees to discuss ethical concerns and dilemmas openly can help identify potential conflicts early on and prevent unethical behavior. This can be achieved through regular training and discussions that promote an inclusive and ethical work culture; for example, using the acronym (PEAR), people, environment, asset, and reputation to assess risk.

Furthermore, diversity and inclusion officers should prioritize building relationships and networks with local stakeholders in different cultural contexts. This allows for a better understanding of local customs, values, and ethical norms, enabling more effective decision-making and conflict resolution.

In addition, it is important to establish effective reporting mechanisms that encourage employees to report ethical concerns without fear of retaliation. This can be achieved through anonymous reporting channels and a robust whistleblower protection policy.

Finally, diversity and inclusion officers should continuously assess and evaluate the effectiveness of their ethical management strategies. Regular audits and assessments can help identify areas for improvement and ensure that ethical guidelines are followed consistently across all business operations.

In conclusion, managing ethical dilemmas in cross-cultural business requires a proactive and culturally sensitive approach. It also requires due diligence and risk assessment of culture and ethics in the organization. By developing intercultural competence, establishing clear ethical guidelines, fostering open communication, building relationships with local stakeholders, and implementing effective reporting mechanisms, diversity and inclusion officers can help create an inclusive and ethically sound business environment in line with the organization's vision. This not only enhances the reputation and integrity of the organization but also promotes a more sustainable and socially responsible business practice.

Overcoming Stereotypes and Prejudices in Global Business

In today's interconnected world, global business opportunities are expanding rapidly. However, with this expansion comes the challenge of navigating cultural differences and overcoming stereotypes and prejudices. Business professionals must develop intercultural competence and learn to embrace diversity to succeed in the global marketplace. This subchapter explores strategies for overcoming stereotypes and prejudices in international business, providing valuable insights for diversity and inclusion officers and intercultural competence professionals.

Understanding Stereotypes and Prejudices

Stereotypes and prejudices are deeply ingrained in human behavior and can hinder effective communication and collaboration in global business. Recognizing that stereotypes are oversimplified generalizations about a particular group of people is crucial, while prejudices are preconceived opinions or attitudes formed without sufficient knowledge or understanding. These biases can lead to misunderstandings, conflicts, and missed business opportunities.

Promoting Intercultural Competence

Intercultural competence is the key to overcoming stereotypes and prejudices in global business. Diversity and inclusion officers are crucial in promoting intercultural competence within organizations aligned with the strategic objectives and vision for business impact. By providing opportunities for intercultural competence assessment, intercultural development plans, follow-on counseling, training programs, workshops, and resources, they can help business professionals develop skills; for example, increased cultural self-understanding and increased focus on understanding cultural differences, recognizing cultural commonality and differences in one's own and other cultures, ability to shift cultural perspective and adapt one's behaviors to cultural context. A qualified assessor assesses these competencies in the Intercultural Development Inventory (IDI). This enables individuals to challenge their own biases and engage effectively with people from different cultural backgrounds.

Breaking Down Stereotypes

One effective strategy for overcoming stereotypes is through education and exposure, but assessment must be first! Business professionals can gain a more nuanced understanding and challenge existing stereotypes by learning about different cultures, their values, traditions, and customs. Encouraging employees to participate in cross-cultural experiences, such as international assignments or cultural immersion programs, can broaden their perspectives and break down stereotypes. A good intercultural development plan can assist with this.

Addressing Prejudices

Addressing prejudices requires creating a safe and inclusive environment where individuals feel comfortable expressing their concerns and engaging in open dialogue. The IDI assessments discussed earlier have high confidentiality for individual debriefings and reporting. The individual and the QA are the only ones with access to the data. In large organizations, there may be liaisons from the organization and several QAs doing assessments for the organization, but assigned QAs still maintain confidentiality. The group reports are generalized and can be helpful for teams. Diversity and inclusion officers can facilitate separate discussions as part of group development plans, mediate conflicts, and promote collaboration among diverse teams. This approach enables addressing and mitigating prejudices through informed, respectful, and confidential conversations, leveraging the insights from IDI assessments.

In conclusion, overcoming stereotypes and prejudices in global business is a continuous journey that requires commitment and effort. Diversity and inclusion officers can help business professionals develop the necessary skills to navigate cultural differences successfully by promoting intercultural competence and providing opportunities for education and exposure. Breaking down stereotypes and addressing prejudices will foster a more inclusive work environment and lead to enhanced collaboration, increased innovation, and improved business outcomes in the global marketplace.

9 TRAINING AND DEVELOPMENT FOR INTERCULTURAL COMPETENCE

Designing Intercultural Training Programs

In today's globalized business world, organizations must develop intercultural competence among their workforce. As Diversity and Inclusion Officers, your role in designing and implementing effective intercultural training programs is crucial in fostering an environment of understanding and collaboration within your organization. This subchapter explores the key considerations and strategies for designing learning and training programs tailored specifically for business professionals seeking to enhance their intercultural competence and align them with the vision for business impact.

The first step in designing intercultural learning and training programs is to assess your organization's needs. Conducting a thorough analysis of the current cultural dynamics, challenges, and goals will help you identify the gaps that must be addressed. This can be done through surveys, focus groups, or interviews with employees at different levels and from diverse backgrounds. It should also be done as part of the organization's overall continuous performance improvement (CPI) process involving strengths, weaknesses, opportunities, and threats (SWOT). This process also examines the competitive environment, gaps, and evaluation system. In talent development, a needs assessment is often the first step in designing training programs. However, a more nuanced approach involves engaging organizations in strategic inquiry. By asking 15-20 carefully crafted questions, one can guide organizations to articulate their competitive landscape, initiatives, and talent development strategies. This collaborative process effectively serves as a self-realized needs assessment, often revealing gaps in their understanding of the competitive environment and alignment of programs. It's important to recognize that solutions extend beyond formal training. For instance, mentoring and coaching are vital avenues for development, offering personalized guidance and support.

Additionally, considering the format of learning interventions is crucial. While in-person workshops offer interactive and experiential learning opportunities, virtual sessions provide flexibility and accessibility, particularly for widespread teams. The format should align with the organization's resources, preferences, and learning objectives. This holistic view of talent development emphasizes that learning is an ongoing process, not confined to structured training sessions but encompassing a range of developmental experiences and modalities.

The impact of learning programs is another critical aspect to consider. Not all solutions require training! Depending on the resources and preferences of your organization, you may choose to conduct in-person workshops, virtual sessions, or a combination of both. In-person workshops allow for direct interaction and experiential learning, while virtual sessions provide flexibility and reach for a geographically dispersed workforce. The first step is an assessment of intercultural competence.

It is essential to incorporate interactive and participatory learning methods. Still, even more important outcomes affect indicators impacting the business and vision to enhance the effectiveness of learning programs. Role plays, simulations, group discussions, and cultural immersion activities can help participants develop empathy, adaptability, critical thinking, and other skills-based strategies needed to help progress toward the vision. Actions, programs, and initiatives should be aligned with performance goals, strategies, mission, purpose, and vision for business impact. Integrating technology, such as online platforms for language learning or virtual reality simulations, can provide immersive and engaging learning experiences.

Evaluation and continuous improvement are integral to the success of intercultural learning programs. Typically, collecting participant feedback through surveys or focus groups will enable you to assess the program's impact and identify areas for improvement. In a system that uses CPI, an evaluation system using Kirkpatrick's Four Levels of Evaluation is likely used as the evaluation system. In this system, level 1 consists of reaction surveys to training (happy/glad), level 2 involves assessments and tests of participants, level 3 application (observed behavior) months later on the job by supervisors, and level 4 business impact like cost-benefit. Phillips Level 5 Return on Investment is also used in the CPI system. Regularly updating (CPI) programs and content to reflect evolving cultural dynamics and incorporating participant feedback will help ensure the program remains relevant and effective over time.

In conclusion, designing intercultural learning and training programs for business professionals is a strategic endeavor that requires a deep understanding of the organization's needs and goals for business impact. By incorporating relevant content, interactive learning methods, and continuous evaluation, you can equip your workforce with the necessary skills and mindset to navigate the complexities of the global business landscape. Fostering intercultural competence will enhance business performance and create an inclusive and harmonious work environment where diversity is celebrated and leveraged for success.

Effective Intercultural Learning Strategies

In today's globalized world, intercultural competence has become essential for business professionals. As diversity and inclusion officers, your role is crucial in fostering a culture that values and celebrates differences. This subchapter will explore effective intercultural learning strategies that can be implemented to develop this competence in business professionals.

1.   **Cultural Immersion**: Encourage individuals to immerse

themselves in different cultures through travel, living abroad, or participating in cultural exchange programs. Experiencing different customs, traditions, and ways of thinking firsthand helps individuals develop a deeper understanding and appreciation for diversity.

2. **Cross-Cultural Training**: Provide comprehensive training programs that cover various aspects of intercultural competence. These programs can include cultural awareness sessions, language classes, and workshops on effective communication across cultures. By equipping professionals with the necessary knowledge and skills, they can navigate cultural differences more effectively.

3. **Cultural Mentoring**: Establish a mentoring program where employees from different cultural backgrounds can guide and support each other. Pairing individuals with mentors with experience in a different culture allows two-way knowledge exchange and fosters empathy and understanding.

4. **Virtual Learning**: Utilize technology to provide virtual learning opportunities. Online courses, webinars, and interactive platforms can offer flexibility and accessibility for individuals to learn independently. These platforms can also facilitate virtual collaborations and discussions among professionals from diverse backgrounds.

5. **Experiential Learning**: Encourage professionals to engage actively in intercultural experiences within their workplace. This can involve participating in international projects, working with diverse teams, or attending conferences and seminars focused on multiculturalism. By applying their knowledge in real-life situations, individuals can enhance their intercultural competence effectively.

6. **Continuous Learning**: Promote a culture of lifelong learning by encouraging professionals to develop their intercultural competence continuously. Provide resources such as books, articles, podcasts, and online forums where individuals can explore different cultures and engage in discussions. Encourage reflection and self-assessment to identify areas for improvement and growth.

As part of the debriefing phase of the intercultural development inventory of your intercultural competence, the intercultural development plan (IDP) is shown to the participants. The participant must design and implement their IDP using the temple provided. It should be several months before participants might retake the assessment. There are many myths about just being exposed to different cultures or immersing in them, which will improve one's assessment score. The IDP asks several questions about your experiences with diverse communities, workplaces, and cultural groups, as well as identifying several goals with performance metrics. Some of the above learning opportunities are mentioned for the IDP, along with theatre, films, arts, books, articles, intercultural coaching, and journals.

By implementing these effective intercultural learning strategies, including assessment, diversity and inclusion officers can help business professionals develop the global mindset necessary to excel in today's multicultural business environment. Remember, intercultural competence is not a one-time achievement but an ongoing journey of learning and growth. The majority (62%) of the scores and levels of individuals who take the IDI are in the middle range (Minimization).

Coaching and Mentoring for Intercultural Competence

Intercultural competence (IC) is a moral imperative and a strategic business advantage. This subchapter explores how effective coaching and mentoring in IC directly translates to measurable business outcomes. These strategies enhance global communication, reduce cross-cultural misunderstandings, and foster successful international partnerships, leading to cost savings and increased ROI. As diversity officers, it's crucial to align IC initiatives with these concrete business objectives, demonstrating the direct correlation between a culturally competent workforce and the organization's bottom line to the C-Suite.

Coaching and mentoring are powerful tools that can guide individuals to develop a global mindset and navigate cultural complexities effectively for business impact. By providing personalized development plans, guidance, and support, coaches, and mentors can help professionals expand their knowledge of different cultures, enhance their cultural self-awareness, and develop the skills to communicate and collaborate across cultures. Enhancing coaching includes personalized insights, alignment with development orientation, focused developmental learning, confidentiality, and alignment with the organization's vision. Some examples of business impact include enhanced global team collaboration and communication leading to productivity, improved relationship-building with international clients, increased Net

Promoter Score, reduced misunderstanding, and increased organizational reputation.

One of the key benefits of coaching and mentoring is the opportunity for individuals to engage in self-reflection and gain a deeper understanding of their own cultural biases and assumptions. Through open and honest conversations, coaches and mentors can challenge these biases and encourage professionals to adopt a more inclusive and empathetic mindset.

Coaches and mentors can also provide concrete strategies and techniques for developing intercultural competence. This may include understanding cultural norms and values, improving communication skills, and developing cultural intelligence. Through regular coaching sessions, professionals can acquire the necessary skills to adapt their behaviors and approaches when working with colleagues and clients from different cultural backgrounds.

Furthermore, coaching and mentoring can help professionals navigate the complexities of cross-cultural relationships and conflicts. By providing a safe and supportive environment, coaches and mentors can guide individuals in understanding and resolving misunderstandings, fostering trust, and building strong relationships across cultures.

Selecting coaches and mentors with a high level of intercultural competence is essential to ensure the effectiveness of coaching and mentoring programs. Often, this likely involves selecting coaches with a higher development level than your own for IDPs. However, with the advent of AI and Open ChatGPT4, coaches can simulate higher level development orientations for coaching solutions. These coaching individuals should have extensive cross-cultural experience and a deep understanding of cultural dynamics in the business context. Additionally, ongoing training and supervision should be provided to coaches and mentors to ensure their skills are up to date and aligned with the evolving needs of the diverse workforce. Accordingly, it would not be uncommon to ask for the coach's certification and qualifications, which are updated and current!

In conclusion, coaching and mentoring are vital in developing intercultural competence among business professionals. By providing personalized guidance and support, coaches and mentors can help individuals embrace cultural diversity, enhance their cultural self-awareness, and develop the skills needed to thrive in a globalized business environment. As diversity and inclusion officers, you can champion the integration of coaching and mentoring programs within your organizations, fostering a culture of intercultural competence and driving business success in an increasingly interconnected world.

Measuring the Impact of Intercultural Training Initiatives

Diversity and inclusion have become crucial for success in today's interconnected global business landscape. As diversity and inclusion officers, your role is to foster intercultural competence among business professionals and ensure that organizations thrive in diverse environments. However, assessing the effectiveness of intercultural training initiatives can be challenging. Done wrongly, one can quickly lose the confidence of executives to deliver business impact aligned with the vision. This subchapter aims to provide valuable insights into measuring the impact of these initiatives, enabling you to enhance intercultural competence in your organization.

Firstly, it is essential to establish clear objectives for intercultural training initiatives. Also, what gets assessed and measured gets done and evaluated. These objectives should align with the organization's overall performance goals, align with the vision, and reflect the business professionals' specific needs. Easier said than done! By setting concrete goals, you can measure the effectiveness of the training initiatives and determine whether they have achieved the desired outcomes. However, to ensure they are aligned with the vision, the CPI process must facilitate validation of the mission and vision. As mentioned, a detailed description, understanding, and intent of the short mission and vision elements capable of producing measurable performance goals or using those previously acquired by the organization. Determine the indicators of those metrics.

One effective method of measuring the impact is through pre- and post-training assessments. These assessments can be surveys, quizzes, or interviews, which evaluate participants' intercultural competence levels before and after the training. If you use the Kirkpatrick and Phillips system, not all levels require 100% evaluation as this is resource intensive. For example, level 1 evaluation is 100%, level 2 is 60%, level 3 is 30%, level 4 is 10-20%, and level 5 is 3-5%. By comparing the results, you can quantify the improvements made and identify any gaps that need to be addressed further.

Another valuable approach is conducting regular individual and team reviews. This involves assessing participants' and teams' contributions to the organization realizing its vision. Some scorecards measure looking back, while some scorecards measure progress towards the future (vision). The book has been talking about alignment in the context of a detailed understanding and intent of the vision. The same methodology for developing the strategy was not discussed. In the book Total Alignment: Tools and Tactics for Streamlining Your Organization by Riaz and Linda Khadem (2017), all of this is laid out in a vision and strategy tree; mission and vision in the middle as the tree, vision tree and branches on the left and strategy tree and branches on the right. The strategies are developed further with specific performance goals. From these two items, vision and strategy tree, detailed performance behaviors and responsibilities can now be formulated as individual and team scorecards; specific behaviors are indicators of progress towards the vision (future looking).

Furthermore, the book by Khadem (2017) lays out vertical and horizontal reviews for accurate reporting and feedback of measured criteria as indicators towards and in alignment with the vision. It is quite detailed, skills- based, and beyond the scope of this subtopic and book; however, it was worth sketching out how alignment might happen, as it has been mentioned several times in this book. Again, what gets measured gets done!

In conclusion, as diversity and inclusion officers, measuring the impact of intercultural training initiatives is crucial for enhancing intercultural competence among business professionals. By establishing clear objectives, conducting pre-and post-training assessments, performing follow-up evaluations, and tracking long-term organizational metrics and progress towards the vision, you can effectively assess the effectiveness and alignment of these initiatives.

This will enable you to make future-ready data-driven decisions, refine learning and training programs, and create a roadmap to intercultural competence in your organization with a global mindset.

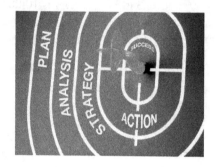

10 THE FUTURE OF INTERCULTURAL COMPETENCE IN BUSINESS

Emerging Trends in Globalization and Diversity

Globalization and diversity have become integral aspects of the business landscape in today's interconnected world. As diversity and inclusion officers, staying updated with the emerging trends in these areas is crucial to navigate the challenges and opportunities effectively they present. Integral aspects mean businesses increasingly engage in various cultures and markets, necessitating a deep understanding of diverse cultural backgrounds (intercultural competence). This subchapter will explore the latest developments in globalization and diversity and their implications for intercultural competence in business. This is required to operate effectively in various international contexts and tap into new markets.

One of the key trends in globalization is the rapid advancement of technology, which has significantly influenced the way businesses operate. The rise of digital platforms and communication tools has made it easier for companies to expand their operations globally, tapping into new markets, innovating, being competitive, and collaborating across borders. This increased connectivity has also facilitated the exchange of ideas and cultures, creating a more diverse and multicultural business environment that fosters improved communications and inclusive environments.

Another emerging trend is the growing significance of emerging markets. Developing economies like China, India, and Brazil are experiencing rapid growth, presenting immense business opportunities. However, operating in these markets requires a deep understanding of their unique cultural, political, and economic dynamics. Intercultural competence is vital for business professionals to successfully navigate the complexities and leverage the potential of these emerging markets.

Furthermore, diversity and inclusion have gained prominence recently as businesses recognize the value of a diverse workforce. Research has consistently shown that diverse teams outperform homogeneous ones, bringing different perspectives and ideas to the table. As diversity and inclusion officers, it is essential to understand the various dimensions of diversity, including race, gender, ethnicity, age, and sexual orientation, and to foster an inclusive culture that embraces and celebrates these differences.

Understanding and valuing emerging trends in diversity and inclusion, the multifaceted aspects of a diverse workforce—such as race, gender, ethnicity, age, and sexual orientation—enhances an organization's ability to connect with a wider range of customers and clients. An inclusive culture attracts and retains top talent from various backgrounds, fostering a work environment conducive to creativity and productivity. This directly contributes to the organization's success, aligning with business goals, strategies, vision, and a deeper understanding of diversity's role in driving innovation and business growth in a global marketplace. Diversity and inclusion officers need to prioritize intercultural competence training for business professionals to navigate these emerging trends in globalization and diversity. This includes developing cultural awareness, knowledge of cultural norms and values, and communication skills to bridge cultural gaps. By doing so, organizations can leverage the benefits of globalization and diversity, foster inclusive workplaces, and gain a competitive advantage in the global marketplace.

The Role of Technology in Intercultural Communication

Technology has become an indispensable tool for intercultural communication in today's globalized world. It has revolutionized how we interact, collaborate, and do business across cultures. This subchapter explores the crucial role of technology in fostering intercultural competence for business professionals, with a specific focus on the perspectives of diversity and inclusion officers.

Technology has enabled individuals and organizations to connect with people from different cultural backgrounds in real time, breaking down geographical barriers. Through video conferencing, instant messaging, and social media platforms, professionals can communicate and collaborate with colleagues and clients from diverse cultures, regardless of physical location. This opens up a world of opportunities for businesses to expand globally and tap into new markets.

Furthermore, technology facilitates the exchange of ideas, knowledge, and information across cultures. Online platforms provide a wealth of resources, such as blogs, forums, and e-learning modules, where professionals can learn about different cultural norms, practices, and communication styles. This knowledge potentially enhances intercultural competence by enabling individuals to adapt their communication and behavior to different cultural contexts, thereby building trust and fostering successful business relationships.

Technology offers unique opportunities for diversity and inclusion officers to promote and support intercultural competence within organizations. Online training programs and webinars can be developed to educate employees on cultural sensitivity, diversity awareness, and inclusive practices. Additionally, technology can be leveraged to create virtual communities and networks where

employees can share experiences, best practices, and challenges related to intercultural communication. This promotes a culture of learning, empathy, and respect within the organization, ultimately enhancing its ability to navigate diverse cultural environments.

However, it is important to acknowledge the limitations and potential pitfalls of relying solely on technology for intercultural communication. While technology provides a convenient and efficient means of communication, it can also lead to misunderstandings and misinterpretations due to the absence of non-verbal cues and contextual information. As such, professionals must be mindful of the limitations and actively seek to complement their online interactions with face-to-face communication whenever possible.

In conclusion, technology is crucial in intercultural communication for business professionals. It enables global connectivity, facilitates knowledge exchange, and supports the development of intercultural competence. Technology offers unique opportunities for diversity and inclusion officers to promote cultural sensitivity and foster inclusive practices within organizations. However, it is vital to recognize the limitations of technology and supplement online interactions with face-to-face communication whenever possible. By embracing technology as a tool and continuously developing intercultural competence, business professionals can navigate the complexities of multicultural environments and thrive in today's globalized world.

Developing a Sustainable Intercultural Competence Strategy

In today's interconnected global business landscape, organizations increasingly recognize the importance of cultivating intercultural competence among their workforce. An interconnected global landscape refers to a world where businesses are increasingly integrated across national borders, influenced by the flow of information, goods, services, and capital on a global scale. This interconnectedness affects a company's mission, vision, and business impact in several ways. As diversity and inclusion officers, you are responsible for creating a sustainable intercultural competence strategy that empowers business professionals to thrive in multicultural environments.

To develop an effective strategy, it is crucial first to understand the concept of intercultural competence, referred to earlier as the ability to navigate and adapt to cultural differences, communicate effectively, and build meaningful relationships across cultures. This skill set is vital for success in international business ventures, as it enables professionals to understand, respect, and leverage cultural diversity to drive innovation, collaboration, and business growth. It is also essential in developing a workforce skilled in understanding and navigating cultural differences; enhancing global cooperation and communication, tailoring products and services to meet diverse cultural needs and preferences, thereby expanding market reach and customer base; and lastly, respecting leveraging cultural diversity contributes to innovation and competitive advantage in the global market.

The first step in developing a sustainable intercultural competence strategy is to assess your organization's current state of intercultural competency. There are a few ways to do this. Engage qualified assessors or conduct your own surveys, interviews, and focus groups to gain insights into employees' intercultural experiences, challenges, and training needs. This data will provide a solid foundation upon which to build your strategy. However, formulating the way ahead should be based on better than just good data.

Next, if feasible, revisit the continuous performance

improvement process as part of being agile, confirm the business environment, and establish clear strategic objectives and performance goals that align with your organization's reviewed values, mission, and vision. These goals or metrics should be SMART goals and the desired outcomes of the intercultural competence strategy, such as increased cross-cultural collaboration, improved communication, and enhanced global leadership. For example, increased participation in cross-cultural training programs by 30% among management staff by Q3 2024; achieve a 25% improvement in intercultural communication effectiveness as measured by employee feedback surveys by the end of 2024; facilitate at least two cross-cultural collaboration projects per department annually; enhance global leadership skills in 50% of senior leaders through specialized coaching by Q3 2024; and conduct quarterly reviews of team collaboration processes to identify and address cultural misunderstandings by the end of each fiscal quarter. These examples might be on the scorecards of individuals and teams responsible for influencing or managing them.

Once the goals are set, design a comprehensive learning or training program that equips business professionals with the necessary knowledge, skills, and attitudes to develop intercultural competence in line with the vision. This program should cover topics such as cultural awareness, cultural intelligence, communication styles, conflict resolution, and global leadership.

To provide practical insights and real-world scenarios, consider incorporating experiential learning methods, such as cross-cultural simulations, role-plays, and case studies. Encourage employees to participate in international assignments, study abroad programs, or virtual exchange programs to gain firsthand experience in different cultural contexts. After assessing their intercultural competence, these should be done in conjunction with intercultural development plans.

To ensure the sustainability of your intercultural competence strategy, establish a support system that includes ongoing coaching, mentoring, and peer-to-peer learning opportunities. Encourage employees to share their intercultural experiences and best practices, fostering a culture of continuous learning and growth.

Measure the impact of your strategy by regularly assessing employees' intercultural competence levels, tracking their progress, and gathering feedback. The business impact of these initiatives must also be tracked and reported, as these will be important to continue to have a seat at the table. Use this data to make necessary adjustments and improvements to your training programs and drive impact.

In conclusion, developing a sustainable intercultural competence strategy, a written one, is essential for organizations striving to thrive in today's global marketplace. As diversity and inclusion officers, you are responsible for designing and implementing an effective strategy that empowers business professionals to navigate cultural differences, communicate effectively, and build successful relationships across cultures. Even though talent development should also have a written strategy, diversity and inclusion should also have one. By investing in intercultural competence, organizations can unlock the full potential of their diverse workforce and gain a competitive advantage globally.

A minimally framed outline for a diversity and inclusion officer's intercultural competence strategy could include the following:

1. **Objectives**: Clear goals aligning with organizational vision and global market demands.

2. **Awareness Programs**: Initiatives to raise cultural awareness within the organization.

3. **Training and Development**: Plans for regular training sessions on cultural intelligence, communication styles, and global leadership.

4. **Evaluation and Feedback**: Mechanisms to assess the strategy's effectiveness and gather feedback.

5. **Continuous Improvement**: Procedures for regularly updating the strategy based on feedback and evolving global trends.

6. **Resource Allocation**: Details of resources allocated for implementing the strategy.

7. **Collaboration with Talent Development**: Integration with broader talent development strategies.

This outline ensures a structured, strategic approach to fostering intercultural competence within the organization. The introduction might also include mission, values, purpose, vision, and strategies which are likely the same or slightly modified from the organization's or talent development, but aligned.

Conclusion: The Journey to Intercultural Excellence

As diversity and inclusion officers, your role in fostering intercultural competence within organizations is crucial. In this subchapter, we conclude the book "The Global Mindset: A Roadmap to Intercultural Competence in Business" by summarizing the key findings and highlighting the journey's significance to intercultural excellence.

Throughout this book, we have explored the concept of intercultural competence and its importance in the ever-evolving global business landscape. We have discussed how developing a global mindset is essential for business professionals to succeed in diverse and multicultural environments. The journey to intercultural excellence requires individuals to navigate cultural differences, adapt communication styles, and build meaningful relationships across cultures.

One of the main takeaways from this book is the recognition that intercultural competence is a lifelong learning process. It is not something that can be achieved overnight or through a one-time training program. It requires continuous self-reflection, curiosity, and a willingness to embrace diverse perspectives.

Intercultural competence goes beyond mere tolerance; it is about actively seeking to understand and appreciate different cultures. By developing this competence, business professionals can effectively navigate complex global markets, build trust with diverse stakeholders, and leverage the power of diversity to drive innovation and growth.

Furthermore, we have emphasized the importance of cultural intelligence (CQ) as a fundamental aspect of intercultural competence. CQ includes adapting to different cultural contexts, understanding cultural norms, and effectively communicating across cultures. Individuals can enhance their ability to collaborate, negotiate, and solve problems in multicultural teams by building CQ.

The journey to intercultural excellence also involves a commitment to inclusive leadership. Inclusive leaders embrace diversity and create an environment where all voices are heard and valued. They foster a culture of inclusivity, where individuals from different cultural backgrounds feel empowered to contribute their unique perspectives and talents.

In conclusion, the journey to intercultural excellence involves a continuous performance improvement, assessment, and evaluation process that requires dedication, self-reflection, and ongoing learning. As diversity and inclusion officers, you play a vital role in promoting intercultural competence within your organizations. By fostering a global mindset, building cultural intelligence, and practicing inclusive leadership, you can create a thriving and inclusive business environment that harnesses the power of diversity for success in the global marketplace aligned with the organization's vision.

ABOUT THE AUTHOR

Dr. William E. Hamilton, Jr., is an accomplished authority in the field of Organizational Development and Leadership, with a deep commitment to fostering cultures of continuous improvement and strategic talent development. Holding a Ph.D. in Organizational Development and Leadership with a specialization in Training and eLearning from the University of Arizona Global Campus, Dr. Hamilton is academically proficient and practically skilled, evident in his role as a Licensed IDI Intercultural Competence Qualified Assessor. As a Certified Professional in Talent Development (CPTD), he has dedicated his career to enriching lives and organizations, harnessing the transformative power of talent development and intercultural competency initiatives. His vision extends beyond traditional frameworks, aiming to create sustainable futures for businesses and individuals alike, driven by a passion for strategic alignment, technology, and talent development.

Dr. Hamilton's robust experience spans over 23 years in the U.S. Navy, in both submarines and combatant ships, where he demonstrated exceptional leadership, technological prowess, and strategic insight. This tenure not only sharpened his operational excellence but also equipped him with a unique blend of discipline and situational awareness, valuable in any high-stakes environment. Dr. Hamilton also worked as a lecturer and trainer in maritime safety at the Malaysian Maritime Academy for over ten years. His role as an Excellence in Practice and Best Awards Judge for the Association for Talent Development and 4o plus submissions has given him a broad perspective on diverse industry talent strategies, enabling him to craft impactful leadership, business, and learning solutions. Dr. Hamilton is well-suited for strategic roles in organizational development, leveraging his extensive background to help guide companies toward effective talent development, performance, and leadership strategies. His commitment to excellence is reflected in his hands-on approach to technology, as evident in web hosting and internet solutions, and his unyielding drive to achieve results that align with business and strategic objectives, making him a standout leader in his field.

Printed in the USA
CPSIA information can be obtained
at www.ICGtesting.com
CBHW062353010824
12554CB00053B/1157

9 798869 247407